MR. CHEAP'S

GUIDE TO

WINE

CHAMPAGNE TASTE ON A BEER BUDGET

Edited by B.A. Cheap

Adams Media
Avon, Massachusetts

Published by
Adams Media, an F+W Publications Company
57 Littlefield Street
Avon, MA 02322
www.adamsmedia.com

ISBN 10: 1-59869-085-X
ISBN 13: 978-1-59869-085-9

Printed in the United States of America.

J I H G F E D C B A

Library of Congress Cataloging-in-Publication Data
is available from the publisher.

Contains portions of material adapted or abridged from *The
Everything® Wine Book, 2nd Edition*, by Beverly Wichman and
Barbara Nowak, © 2005, F+W Publications, Inc.

This publication is designed to provide accurate and authorita-
tive information with regard to the subject matter covered. It is
sold with the understanding that the publisher is not engaged
in rendering legal, accounting, or other professional advice. If
legal advice or other expert assistance is required, the services of
a competent professional person should be sought.

—From a *Declaration of Principles* jointly adopted by
a Committee of the American Bar Association
and a Committee of Publishers and Associations

Many of the designations used by manufacturers and sellers to
distinguish their product are claimed as trademarks. Where
those designations appear in this book and Adams Media was
aware of a trademark claim, the designations have been printed
with initial capital letters.

*This book is available at quantity discounts for bulk purchases.
For information, please call 1-800-872-5627.*

contents

acknowledgments

The editor kindly thanks Anita and Todd Lees, wine connoisseurs and savvy wine bargain shoppers, for their expert input. Also, Brian Ballerini, Marjorie Myers, Marian Selip, and Brett Aved for their consultations and support.

THE BENEFIT$ OF BEING "CHEAP"

Welcome to the world of Mr. Cheap! What exactly does my world entail? In short, drinking great wines at bargain-basement prices—yes, that is possible, I promise.

I know how your typical wine shopping trip unfolds—you enter a liquor store to buy a bottle of wine for a friend's dinner party. You want something that tastes good—but you can't afford to spend a fortune. You scan hundreds of bottles, aisle after aisle . . . how should you choose? By grape type? By vineyard location? By label design? Should you immediately pick a wine priced at the top of your budget (because it must taste better, of course)?

Relax. I'm here to help you avoid that moment of panic and find a cheap bottle of wine that you won't be embarrassed to buy or serve. Although the word *cheap* can have negative connotations, I actually embrace the word. After all, I may be cheap, but I'm not someone who settles for wine that's barely drinkable just because it's inexpensive. No, no, no—I like high-quality wine but I am also a smart shopper. I eschew people who become wine snobs and then recklessly spend more than they need to on wine just to impress their neighbors, guests, or clients. The wine I buy is just as good as what they buy—but it's a fraction of the cost.

After years of extensive research (and a hangover or two), I have developed a strategy for buying wine that allows me to enjoy great wines but still pay my mortgage. And guess what? It's not very difficult. You don't need to travel far and wide. You don't need a tastevin, one of those big, shiny shallow cups that wine stewards in restaurants wear around their necks. You just need to know a little bit about wine—how it's made, where it's made, and how it's priced.

Luckily for you and me, the number of wine producers has more than quadrupled in the last twenty years and new wineries are springing up around the world—making it very possible to expand your wine repertoire but *not* spend a fortune. Want an amazing bottle of Champagne for around $10? See page 217. Need a great Cabernet Sauvignon for under $20? See pages 107, 124, and 147. This book is full of all kinds of insider tips and tricks to help you recognize terrific deals when you see them.

Try to learn as much as possible about wine—a savvy buyer is an educated buyer. And an educated buyer gets the best deals! I want you to become so adept in the world of wines that you'll be able to score wine that tickles the palette, impresses your guests, and doesn't flatten your wallet.

Without further ado, let's get to it. Bottoms up!

chapter 1

AN ABBREVIATED HISTORY OF WINE

. . . .

No only really knows whether humans ingeniously invented or stumbled upon fermented grapes that had turned into a delicious and intoxicating drink. Anthropologists have, however, unearthed evidence that people have been imbibing wine since at least 4000 B.C., and maybe as far back as 6000 B.C., and maybe even further back than that.

. . . .

WINE IN THE ANCIENT WORLD

Wine historians believe Mesopotamia (Persia), near present-day Iran, and Egypt—the end-points of the Fertile Crescent—may have been the birthplace of ancient winemaking; yet recent discoveries point to winemaking in China during the same period.

According to a Persian fable, an ancient king kept his beloved grapes in an earthen jar labeled "poison." Seeking to commit suicide, an unhappy member of his harem drank juice from the jar only to discover that—instead of killing her—the poison completely rejuvenated her spirits. When she shared this knowledge with her king, he took her into his favor and decreed that, henceforth, grapes would be allowed to ferment to the point they became rejuvenating spirits. The grape varieties they used to make wine are believed to be the precursors of those we use today.

The ancient Egyptians cultivated grapes and developed the first arbors and pruning methods. Grapes were stomped and fermented in large wooden vats. The wine was mostly sweet white wine, probably made from the grape we now know as the Muscat of Alexandria. As a matter of respect to the gods, the Egyptians used wine in their funeral rites. Depending on the status held by the deceased, his body and belongings were anointed with wine prior to being entombed.

Phoenicians, who sailed the Mediterranean from what is now the coast of Lebanon, probably introduced the grapevine—and wine—to Greece, Sicily, and north-central Italy.

Thank You, Dionysus!

Greeks embraced wine drinking more enthusiastically than any culture before them. It is said that of all the vessels Greeks used daily, more than half related to the consumption of wine. Wine was considered to be a gift from Dionysus, the patron god and symbol of wine, and was used in religious rituals. Wine was used in commerce. And Greek doctors, including Hippocrates, prescribed it for their patients.

Greeks considered it barbaric to drink wine straight, so they diluted it in varying proportions with water. They also typically stored their wine in porous clay jugs, which had to be sealed to preserve the wine. They caulked the jugs with the resin of pine trees, which imparted its unique essence, and which eventually morphed into the traditional Greek wine Retsina.

Wine was important to the economies of Greek cities. It was traded within Greece and exported throughout the Mediterranean world. As Greece began to colonize the western Mediterranean, the Greeks took their grapevines and winemaking technology with them.

The Romans Conquer Wine

At its greatest outward expansion, the Roman Empire included most of the Mediterranean lands and a good part of Europe, where grapes were already under cultivation. The Romans fostered development and around 1000 B.C. began classifying grape varieties, charting ripening characteristics, identifying diseases, and increasing yields through irrigation and fertilization. They developed wooden barrels to store the wines in place of the skins and jars previously used. And, as glass blowing became more common, the Romans may have been the first ones to put wine into glass containers.

By the first century A.D., each Roman citizen drank half a liter each day. Winemaking techniques had spread from Italy to Spain, Germany, England, and France, and those regions developed their own vineyards, creating a wine boom! The supply (or oversupply) of wine drove down the prices—so much so that Emperor Domitian ordered the great vineyards of France be uprooted to eliminate the competition. Fortunately that order wasn't fully executed, and it was officially rescinded two centuries later. When the Roman Empire fell for good in 476, the great wine regions of Europe were covered with potent vines.

WINE IN MEDIEVAL EUROPE

Wine and its extraordinary properties have always been associated with spirituality and religion. While most of the religions practiced in the eastern Mediterranean incorporated wine in their rituals, the spread of Christianity in the fourth century ensured the survival of viticulture and winemaking after the collapse of the Roman Empire. Monasteries and cathedrals that sprang up across Europe amassed substantial vineyard holdings. The monks—who had the education, the financial resources of the Catholic Church, and the requisite time for cultivating land and trying new techniques—became some of the most important winemakers of the Middle Ages. Monastic wineries in Burgundy, Bordeaux, Champagne, the Loire Valley, and the Rhone Valley helped France emerge as the pre-eminent winemaking region in the world.

WINE IN THE NEW WORLD

With the discovery and colonization of new lands, emigrating Europeans took their vines and their winemaking knowledge elsewhere. Exploration and settlement brought wine to the Americas and South Africa in the 1500s and 1600s and to Australia in the 1700s. The wine

MR. CHEAP'S GUIDE TO WINE

history of Europe thus became intertwined—for better and for worse—with that of the New World.

Spanish Conquistadors

When Hernando Cortés defeated the Aztecs in 1521, he immediately directed all new Spanish settlers to plant vines on the land they'd been granted. Winemaking flourished to such an extent that the settlers needed to import less and less wine from Spain. As a result, the king of Spain levied heavy taxes and ordered vineyards destroyed in all of Spain's new colonies. The edict was enforced most aggressively in Mexico, and the growth of the burgeoning wine industry there came to an abrupt halt.

The church was the sole exception to the king's edict. Just like in Europe, vineyards survived under the care of the church. Missions—particularly, Jesuit missions—were established early in Chile, Argentina, Peru, and Mexico. Later, a series of missions along the Pacific Coast would bring winemaking to California.

Dying on the Vine

In America, early settlers discovered that the native vines were not like those they were familiar with back in Europe. Being pioneers, they forged ahead and fermented anyway. The colonists imported vine cuttings of Vitis vinifera from Europe—Cabernet Sauvignon, Merlot, Chardonnay. All up and down the Atlantic coast settlers planted vines from every great European wine region. Even Thomas Jefferson, the wine geek of his era, planted vines at Monticello. No one succeeded. Each vineyard would die off after only two or three years. It was thought that the extremes of weather were the reason for failure. Or perhaps that indigenous diseases were at fault. A hundred years later, another possible cause came to light—the dreaded phylloxera.

Even though the vinifera vines failed, these experiments in the 1800s led to the emergence of new American varieties. It's generally assumed that they were produced by chance through pollen exchange between the vinifera and earlier American varieties. These hybrids became the foundation for the wine industry in the eastern United States. Winemaking centers emerged in Ohio, Missouri, on the shores of Lake Erie, and in the Finger Lakes region of upstate New York.

Mission: Cultivating Grapes

Beginning around 1770, Franciscan monks established missions—and planted vineyards—up the coast of what would become California. Father Junípero Serra led the way when he planted the first vineyard at Mission San Diego. He traveled north and established eight more missions, which earned him the moniker "father of California wine."

The Gold Rush of 1849 brought frenzied growth in California. Sonoma soon had 22,000 acres under vine, and Napa had 18,000. The Santa Clara Valley and Livermore Valley were widely planted and had numerous wineries at this same time. Many pioneer vintners settled south and east of the San Francisco Bay where most of the bottling plants were located. Railroads arrived, and by the end of the century, California had become the premier wine-growing region in the country.

A Lousy Development

In 1863 an unidentified vine disease in France's Rhone Valley had spread to Provence. By the late 1860s vineyards all over France began dying. And over the next twenty years it decimated nearly all the vineyards of Europe. Why? The scourge *phylloxera* generated from a louse indigenous to the eastern United States. Barely

MR. CHEAP'S GUIDE TO WINE

visible to the naked eye, it sucked the nutrients from the roots of grapevines and slowly starved the vines. Native American grapevines had a thick and tough root bark and suffered no damage from this sucking parasite. But vinifera vines had no such evolutionary protection.

Through the Grapevine

beware of hitchhikers
Between 1858 and 1862 large numbers of rooted American vines were sent to Bordeaux, England, Ireland, Alsace, Germany, and Portugal. Unfortunately, phylloxera the villainous probably hitched a ride.

The parasite spread and affected vines in California, Australia, New Zealand, and South Africa. For a while, eradicating phylloxera seemed hopeless. Eventually a solution presented itself: graft vinifera vines to pest-resistant American rootstocks. It worked, but grafting and replanting each and every vine in Europe proved long and laborious.

AMERICAN WINERIES DRY UP

The winemaking business had its ups and downs— sometimes due to insects and other times to economics. But in 1920 it crashed and burned because of politics. The Prohibition movement in America wasn't a sudden twentieth-century phenomenon. It started county-by-county, state-by-state, and steadily grew. By the outbreak of World War I, thirty-three states had gone dry.

The Eighteenth Amendment was ratified on January 29, 1919, and one year later Prohibition began, making virtually all alcoholic beverages illegal. Even after ratification by the states, the amendment still needed an act of

Congress to make it enforceable. That came in the form of the Volstead Act, in which Minnesota Congressman Volstead defined intoxicating liquors as any beverage containing more than one-half of 1 percent alcohol.

A Crushing Blow

The American wine industry was soon decimated. Growers and producers—if they didn't go completely under—had to find creative ways to stay in business. They could make cooking wine, as long as it was salted and undrinkable. Sacramental and religious wines were permitted and somehow found their way to secular markets. Because it wasn't for "beverage purposes," medicinal alcohol remained legal, and doctors began prescribing more and more of it. Home producers were permitted to make up to 200 gallons of wine a year.

By 1933, when the Twenty-first Amendment repealed Prohibition, the country had lost its winemakers and an entire generation of wine drinkers. By 1936, fifteen states had laws that created state monopolies on wine sales and prevented free-market competition. Other states, while allowing hotels and restaurants to serve wine, banned bars and "liquor by the drink." And still other states left serving and selling options to local jurisdictions. The aftermath of Prohibition created a hodgepodge of laws that vary from state to state and community to community.

WINE IN THE USA!

As the wine industry rebuilt itself after the repeal of Prohibition, it found a market much changed in its thirteen-year hiatus. The quality of wine was very poor, in part because California grape growers were raising grapes that shipped well, rather than grapes that made fine wine. Wineries mostly sold their wines to wholesalers who bottled them under their own brands and then, in turn, sold them under generic names like Chablis and Burgundy. Nevertheless, the American wine industry slowly recovered.

Merci Beaucoup

French hybrids crossed American and European vines to resist phylloxera. These resultant new varieties were hardy enough to withstand a northeastern winter, yet yielded good-quality wine without the "grapey" taste of many native varieties.

The American wine boom really began, however, with the affluence of the late 1950s. Educated suburbanites, especially those wealthy enough to travel abroad, embraced wine and soon began equating it with *savoir faire*. Wine, which to most of the wine-drinking world was a simple beverage, soon became a status symbol in the United States.

Through the Grapevine

slipping under the radar . . . american style

Some ingenious California grape growers introduced a product they named Vine-Glo. While they weren't permitted to make wine, the growers could still make grape juice. They sold their juice with instructional material telling consumers what not to do—lest their juice turn to wine in sixty days!

A few potent role models helped. When John F. Kennedy was sworn in he brought a new sense of internationalism—along with his wife, Jackie, who loved all things French. French restaurants—and French wines—became very trendy. And from a kitchen in a Boston television studio, Julia Child taught a generation of Americans how to prepare French cuisine, and how to match it with French wine.

Meanwhile, California's reputation for world-class fine wines rapidly grew. In the early 1970s, resourceful winemakers, many educated in their craft at the University of California at Davis, developed a whole new genre of California wine—high-alcohol, fruity wine that took full advantage of the long California growing season. In a blind tasting that pitted several California wines against top French wines in 1976, the American wines—Stags' Leap Cabernet and Château Montelena Chardonnay—won. The decision, by a panel comprised of all French judges, shocked the world.

Through the Grapevine

prize-winning grandfathers

Despite all the hype surrounding it at the time, topping French wines in a 1976 competition was not a first for American wines. In 1880, Charles Wetmore, California's first Commissioner of Agriculture, brought cuttings from France to California. In 1889, he sent the first wine from these vines to the Gran Prix in Paris, where it won top honors. And after Prohibition in 1939, Wente Bros. sent a wine to the same world wine tasting and also won the Gran Prix.

Doing It Our Way

In distinct contrast to the European winemakers' custom of naming their wines after the place where they were produced, American winemakers began labeling their wines according to the grape variety. And

Americans soon became attached to their new varietals: Cabernet Sauvignon, Merlot, Sauvignon Blanc. Bob Trinchero, owner of Sutter Home Winery was the first to make a fruity, pink, slightly sweet Rosé that became an instant and enormous success in the American market. Its popularity helped to drive yearly wine consumption in the United States up to two gallons per person.

Sharing the Joy

A boom in wine production happened in areas far removed from California. Historical wine regions like New York and Ohio experienced intense growth after a long period of relative dormancy. Areas that had modest wine production in the past picked up speed. Wines from Texas, Virginia, Pennsylvania, and New Mexico—to name a few—became commonplace. The Northwest underwent significant planting, and soon Oregon and Washington developed outstanding reputations for their wines. Today, every state in the Union has a winery!

CURRENT TRENDS IN WINE PREFERENCES

As wine-drinking Americans, we've upgraded our taste in wines. The proliferation of wine classes, wine tastings, dinners, and publications has helped. A White Zin craze morphed into a Chardonnay trend and Merlot fad. And now there are "newer" fashions: Pinot Noir (particularly after the popularity of the movie *Sideways*), Pinot Grigio, and Shiraz, for example. Today, California likes Old World "Cal-Ital" varieties like Barbera and Sangiovese, Syrah, and Grenache—the traditional grapes of the Rhone Valley of France.

global update

According to Oz Clarke, wine critic and author, high-quality, inexpensive wines can be found in ripening international markets. South America—Chile in particular—is climbing the charts with their Merlot, Cabernet, Pinot, Shiraz, and cool-weather whites. Argentina and Uruguay are also picking up steam. In Europe, Greece is churning out revolutionary wines, while Portugal and Spanish reds are also deepening into velvety wines. And you can readily find these wines at very affordable prices.

International collaboration as well as international competition have picked up. Famous names in wine—Mondavi, Lafite Rothschild, Lapostolle—have invested heavily in land and facilities in places like South America to produce high-quality wines. On the other hand, Australian wineries are giving American producers a run for their money with well-made inexpensive wines. They've been so successful that some U.S. wineries are labeling their bottles of Syrah with the Aussie name, Shiraz.

chapter 2

DIFFERENT TYPES OF WINE

. . . .

After seeing Lucy in old TV reruns sprawled out in a vat of gooey red pulp with grape stains up to her knees, it can be a tad difficult to take the crushing of grapes seriously. But, like all winemaking processes, it's very serious business. Every wine-making process has a direct effect on what we drink: whether the wine is red or white or pink; whether it's sweet or dry; whether it has bubbles, oak, or tannins; and even how much alcohol it contains. All these remarkable traits are intentionally created on their fascinating journey from grape to glass.

. . . .

FROM VINE TO GRAPE TO WINE!

When you think about it, winemaking is pretty basic. It's almost as if the grapes themselves want to be turned into wine. Wine grapes will grow almost anyplace that has a warm to temperate climate. Ripe grapes contain lots of sugar. And the skins of the grapes are the perfect surface for natural yeasts to thrive. All the conditions you need to make wine.

First you pick a bunch of ripe grapes and crush them. Crushing releases the sugar inside the grapes and causes the yeast to come in contact with the sugar. The yeast "eats" the sugar and turns it into alcohol and carbon dioxide. The process is called *fermentation*, and it transforms plain old grape juice into sublime wine.

When nature is in balance, all goes according to plan. The reality, of course, is that nature can be annoyingly unpredictable, and a winemaker can run into a plethora of problems in the quest to produce an outstanding bottle of wine. Fortunately, technology has come to the aid of winemakers in an activity that is a careful balance of art and science.

There are many technological options available to the modern winemaker. But—whether the end product is red, white, or pink, or whether it's cheap or expensive—there are several principles common to all winemaking.

No Vine Before Its Time

The quality of a wine depends, first and foremost, on the grapes, which have to be picked at the precise moment of ripeness. As grapes ripen, the sugar content increases. At the same time, their acidity declines. The trick is to harvest them when the sugar and acid levels are in balance. This is always a subjective judgment by the winemaker and is based on what style of wine he is producing.

when is a wine a bargain?
- When it is equal to or better than many wines at twice the price.
- When it is a very drinkable wine at everyday drinkable prices.
- When it is a wine you adore at a special price.
- When it is an outstanding wine at clearance prices.

It's crucial that the grapes are picked and transported to the winery without prematurely splitting the skins. While handpicking is best, mechanical harvesting machines can handle grape bunches with care. This equipment tenderly squeezes the juice from the grapes so that the bitter seeds aren't crushed. The resulting substance is called *must*—a combination of juice, skins, and seeds. Depending on what kind of wine is being produced, the skins and seeds are either discarded or left in for a period of time.

How They Do What They Do

Winemakers can "manage" fermentation to enhance the resulting wine. Fermentation usually takes place in large stainless steel tanks, but winemakers can choose to substitute oak barrels to add flavor and complexity. Because high temperatures kill yeast and end fermentation, winemakers control the temperature through refrigeration and circulation. Instead of relying solely on naturally occurring yeasts, they can add cultured yeasts to the juice that are better suited to the kind of wine they're producing. For wines that have fermented with their skins, winemakers decide the appropriate time to separate the skins from the liquid.

sweet nothings

If a wine is fully fermented to produce a dry wine,
about 40 percent of the grapes' sugar is converted to
carbon dioxide and about 60 percent becomes alcohol.
If all the sugar is not converted, you get a low-alcohol
wine that will have some degree of sweetness. The leftover sugar, called *residual sugar*, determines how sweet
a wine will be.

When grapes don't fully ripen and lack enough
natural grape sugar to produce reasonable alcohol levels,
the winemaker can add sugar to the juice. This practice, called *chaptalization*, is illegal in some winemaking
areas—Italy and California, to name two—but perfectly
allowable in France and other U.S. states.

After fermentation, coarse sediment particles called
lees settle at the bottom of the fermentation vessel. This
sludgelike material is made up of dead yeast cells and
small grape particles. The wine is usually separated from
the lees when fermentation has run its course. But a
winemaker can choose to extend the lees contact for further aging to produce a wine with more complexity. This
is more often done with white wines than with reds.

Wines, by nature, are cloudy because of the dead
yeast and tiny particulate matter. Once fermentation
is complete, most wines are clarified by *fining*, a process that removes those microscopic elements. When
fining agents—such as charcoal, bentonite clay, casein
(milk protein), or egg whites—are added to the wine,
they grab onto the solid particles and drag them, over
a period of days, to the bottom of the tank. The wine
can then be separated from the sediment by *racking*, the
siphoning off of the clear juice. Some winemakers will

further clarify the wine right before bottling by filtering it through layers of paper filters or synthetic fiber mesh.

Sometimes, between fermentation and aging, a winemaker will add special bacteria to encourage an extra fermentation called *malolactic fermentation*—ML or MLF, for short. This process makes the wine less acidic. It converts malic acid in the wine, which has a sharp taste, to lactic acid, which gives the wine a creamy or buttery flavor. In terms of what you sense in your mouth, imagine an apple at one end of the spectrum and milk at the other. Most reds and some whites undergo MLF.

Through the Grapevine

no clarification necessary

Some winemakers think that fining and filtering remove too much flavor and body from the wine, and forego those processes. The resultant wines (sometimes, but not always, labeled "unfined" and "unfiltered") may have a small amount of sediment in the bottle, but the winemakers believe a fuller flavor will more than offset any inconvenience to the consumer.

Roll Out the Barrel

After fermentation, some wines are ready for immediate bottling. Rosés, many whites, and light reds are bottled soon after fermentation and should be drunk while still young. Others will be aged—either in stainless steel or oak—for several months or up to several years. Fine red wines, in particular, need to age to reach their full potential. This is accomplished in oak barrels, which allows the wines to soften and absorb some of the wood's flavors and tannins.

capping it off

Grape skins rise to the top of the fermenting must, forming a "cap" over the juice. This cap needs to be broken up and mixed back in to extract the desirable qualities from the skins. The cap is pumped or manually punched back with a paddle. A "punched-cap" wine, it's said, reflects the winemaker—a big, strong winemaker will force more extract from the skins, resulting in a big, highly tannic wine.

Many wines, both red and white, are blends. Before bottling, a winemaker may combine several different grape varieties—like adding some Merlot to some Cabernet Sauvignon—or different barrels (or *lots*) of the same wine in order to make the best-tasting bottle of wine.

Bottle Brigade!

When a wine is ready for release, it's bottled in a highly mechanized process that keeps the wine from contact with the air, germs, and impurities. Sparkling clean bottles are filled, corked, capped, and labeled with little human intervention. For the finest wines it is often advantageous for the winery to keep the bottles in storage for two or more years. This makes for better wine when it finally reaches the market and, in many cases, substantially increases the value of the wine.

RUBY REDS

All grapes, regardless of color, have the same greenish pulp and colorless juice. So where does a red wine get its color? The skins. Red wine grapes are crushed leaving the juice, skins, seeds, and, sometimes, stems together in the fermenting vat, during which time the skins impart their color and tannins to the juice.

When fermentation is complete—one to three weeks later—the new wine is drawn from the vat. This first run of juice, called *free-run juice*, comes forth voluntarily. Afterward, the mixture is pressed, yielding *press wine*, which is darker and more tannic. The winemaker may, at this point, choose to blend the two in order to adjust the tannin level. Now the wine is clarified and transferred to either oak barrels for aging or stainless steel vats for holding in an oxygen-free environment.

Barrel vs. Bottle Aging

Prolonged barrel aging before bottling is desirable for most types of red wine to allow all the flavor components time to harmonize. The oak barrel imparts flavor to the wine, sometimes reminiscent of vanilla or wood (surprise!) and other times described as spicy. The barrel also allows a very slight and controlled exposure to oxygen. Winemakers usually try to avoid exposing their wines to the air. But this low-level oxidation is actually beneficial to the structure and character of the wine.

$OMMELIER CENTS

a chip off the old barrel

Oak barrels are expensive and usually reserved for premium wines. But wineries sometimes use less-expensive techniques for their cheaper wines, like adding oak chips to the wine in the tanks. If you see an inexpensive wine labeled "oaked" with no mention of "barrel," you can be pretty sure no barrel was used, but often the oak chips sufficiently flavor the wines, making them almost as tasty as barrel-aged wines at more affordable prices.

Some wines improve with further aging in the bottle—particularly fine reds that begin life high in tannins. They include California Cabernet Sauvignon and Zinfandel, French Bordeaux and Italian Barolo—and they can continue to improve after many years and, sometimes, even decades. Their harsh tannins soften. Their aromas become more complex. And their textures become silky.

CRISP WHITES

Because the juice of all grapes is colorless, white wine can be made from any kind of grape. In practice, though, most whites come from "white" grapes—which are actually greenish, greenish yellow, golden yellow, or pinkish yellow.

Through the Grapevine

icy diamonds

White wines have a propensity to produce crystals known as "wine diamonds." They're harmless—but a nuisance. They form from tartaric acid and potassium (both naturally occurring in grapes) that bind together when wine gets too cold. Many winemakers force crystals to form under extremely cold conditions during fermentation so they can remove them. The process is called *cold stabilization.*

In contrast to making red wine, the juice for white wine is fermented without the skins and seeds. The result: no tannins and little color. White wines can take on a pale straw color or greenish to deep gold tones depending on the grape variety and aging treatment.

In making red wines, malolactic fermentation is a given. With white wines it's an option. A winemaker can choose to perform it or not. When you peruse wine shelves, you'll be able to find clean, crisp whites that have not undergone any MLF, full-bodied whites that have undergone full MLF, and whites somewhere in the middle.

Winemakers have similar decisions to make regarding aging white wines in oak barrels. Chardonnay, for example, can benefit from oak. Others such as Riesling and Sauvignon Blanc rarely do.

Most vintners design white wines to be drunk young, but there are exceptions. Some age-worthy whites are white Burgundies, white Bordeaux, and German and Alsace Rieslings.

A ROSÉ IS A ROSÉ IS A ROSÉ

Rosé is French for "pink." And that's how you identify a Rosé wine: by its color. The preferred method for producing Rosés is to crush red wine grapes but allow the skins to sit with the juice for only a short time before separating the juice—anywhere from a few hours to several days. Just long enough to kiss the juice with color. It's the winemaker who determines how long the kiss will last. When the color is to the producer's liking, the winemaking process continues as it would for white wine. An alternative technique involves adding a small amount of finished red wine to a white wine. However, the result is more like a tinted white and has a different taste than a true Rosé.

Rosés have always been drunk in southern France. Originally they were made from leftover grapes that didn't make it into the local red wine. But the winemaking philosophy has changed, and Rosés are now being made on purpose and have acquired respect. They're made in a dry style.

Some of the best Rosés come from France—from Tavel (which makes *only* Rosé wines) in the Rhone region and Anjou in the Loire Valley. Enter *blush wine* in the '80s—same concept, different term. It was a marketing success. White Zinfandel—the first blush wine introduced—became all the rage and spawned many other pinks-from-reds: white Grenache, Merlot Blanc, Cabernet Blanc. Most of them are low in alcohol and sweet, which led to the perception that all Rosés are sweet. In fact, many are dry and off-dry.

$OMMELIER CENTS

preserving your rosés

Even though a Rosé has acidity and tannins acquired from the grape skins, its fruit flavor disappears quickly—which is why you should always buy the most recent vintage available. And, like a white wine, a Rosé should be served well chilled. Keep in mind that Rosés tend to be people and food friendly, and often cost much less than traditional varietals such as cabernet and chardonnay.

Rosé wines can be found by other names. Rosado is a Rosé from Spain. Rosato is a Rosé from Italy. Vin Gris ("gray wine"), from France, is a very pale Rosé made from very lightly pressed red grapes.

SPARKLING BUBBLIES

What a difference a few bubbles make! Sparkling wine starts out as still wine and then undergoes a second fermentation. More carbon dioxide is formed—but, this time, it's captured and not allowed to escape. Et voilà!— a party ready to happen.

There are all sorts of sparkling wines: Cava (from Spain); Prosecco and Asti (from Italy); Sekt (from Germany); blanc de noir (from the Pinot Noir grape); blanc de blanc (from the Chardonnay grape)—and, the most famous, Champagne. Not all sparkling wines are Champagne. In order to legitimately be called Champagne, a sparkling wine must meet the following criteria. It must:

- Be produced in the Champagne district of France.
- Be produced from the Chardonnay, Pinot Noir, and/or Pinot Meunier grapes grown there.
- Get its bubbles via the *méthode champenoise* (Champagne method).

The Champagne method is an expensive and labor-intensive means of naturally carbonating a wine. First, wine is made from local grapes. This is no easy feat. The vineyards of Champagne lie so far north that ripeness is an issue in most years. After clarification and a measure of aging, the wine is put into thick Champagne bottles, along with enough yeast and sugar to initiate a second fermentation. It is this second fermentation in the tightly sealed bottle that puts the bubbles in the bubbly. The carbon dioxide can't get out, so it's dissolved in the wine.

The wine is aged—sometimes for years—along with the dead yeast that accumulates as sediment. The trick is to get rid of the sediment without losing all the bubbles. By gradually tilting the bottle a little bit each day until it is inverted, the dead yeast is coaxed into the neck of the bottle where it can quickly be removed. At that time, the bottle is topped off and adjusted for sweetness and then immediately corked so that the wine doesn't lose its effervescence.

The Champagne method, because it's so time-consuming and labor-intensive, is expensive—one reason for the high price tag of Champagne. Sparkling wines that are carbonated in other, cheaper ways can be sold for much less.

FORTIFIED WINE

Fortified means that extra alcohol has been added to a wine. In the beginning it was done to preserve the wine for shipping, but fortified wines have become specialties to be enjoyed on their own terms.

If you were making regular table wine, you'd crush the grapes and let fermentation take its course. You'd end up with a dry wine with about 12 percent alcohol. For a fortified wine you would add a brandy (usually made from the same grape as the wine) or a neutral spirit. If you add the brandy after fermentation, the fortified wine is dry, with no residual sugar. If it is added before fermentation is complete—before all the natural fruit sugar is consumed—the alcohol stops the yeast from converting the sugars, and you have a sweet fortified wine.

Through the Grapevine

stability plus

The alcohol level of a table wine in the United States, as mandated by government regulations, is 7 to 14 percent. Fortified wines generally have between 17 and 21 percent alcohol. As a result, they're more stable than table wines and less apt to spoil once they've been opened.

There are four primary types of fortified wines: Port, Sherry, Madeira, and Marsala. The popular drinking wines are Port and Sherry. Madeira and Marsala are better known as cooking wines, but there are good bottles of each for drinking.

- Port is sweet and is most often served after a meal. True Port comes from the Douro Valley in Portugal.
- Sherry, from the vineyards of southern Spain, can range from dry to sweet. Pale, dry Sherry is served chilled as an apéritif. Darker, sweet Sherry is usually enjoyed as an after-dinner drink.
- Madeira is named after its birthplace, a Portuguese island off the coast of Africa. Unlike other fortified wines, Madeira is heated in its production. It can be sweet or dry.
- Marsala, named for the town on the western tip of Sicily, comes both dry and sweet. Of all the fortified wines, Marsala is the least distinctive as a beverage and is mostly used for cooking.

JUST DESSERTS

Dessert wines are called "dessert" because, well, they're sweet. They're served either with dessert or as dessert. Timing is everything when it comes to making a dessert wine. The time you pick the grapes, that is. The grapes are harvested very late in the growing season when they're ripe, ripe, ripe. Because of the high concentration of sugar, not all of it converts to alcohol during fermentation. The result is that the wine is extremely sweet. At the same time, the overabundance of sugar means the wine can ferment to a high level of alcohol. The high sugar content also helps preserve the wine so it can improve in the bottle for years.

Exactly how long the grapes are left on the vine before picking is determined by what wines are being produced. Grapes that are harvested late in the season produce *late harvest* wines. The grapes can be left on the vine even longer until they shrivel up and their flavors become concentrated. German wines labeled Auslese, Beerenauslese, and Trockenbeerenauslese come from these grapes.

Other wines—notably Sauternes, Barsac, Tokay, and many California late harvest wines—are produced from grapes that have been allowed to develop a mold (*Botrytis cinerea*). Endearingly called *noble rot*, this mold concentrates the grapes' flavors and adds some of its own.

Grapes, especially those from northern vineyards, can be left on the vine until they freeze. They're picked and pressed before they can thaw, separating out the frozen water and leaving concentrated juice. These are made into *ice wines*.

KEEPING IT KOSHER

Wine has played an important part in Jewish tradition and rituals for thousands of years. Most important religious ceremonies begin with the Kiddush, the prayer over the wine. During Passover, celebrants drink four cups of wine to symbolize the four dimensions of freedom. In ancient times, before the Roman conquest drove the Jewish inhabitants out of what is now Israel, vineyards and winemaking were common. Because tradition mandated the drinking of wine, Jewish winemakers took their skills with them into exile.

When Jewish immigrants settled in the Northeast United States a century ago, the only grapes available to them were the native American Concord grapes. The wines made from these grapes were very high in acid and had a musty character, often referred to as "foxy."

In order to make them palatable, the wines had to be heavily sweetened. This heavy and cloyingly sweet style became synonymous with kosher wine. But it's not a religious dictate. Kosher wines can be—and are—made from any variety of grapes. Since the mid-1980s, kosher winemaking has changed. Kosher wines are increasingly made from popular grape varietals like Chardonnay, Merlot, and Cabernet Sauvignon.

Through the Grapevine

positively juicy

To get a taste of an American "grapey" wine, you need look no further than Manischewitz. It produces the sweet style of kosher wine from the indigenous American Concord grape. It's the same grape used to make grape juice and jelly.

What Does Kosher Mean?

It's Hebrew for good, fitting, or proper. According to Jewish dietary code, foods can be naturally kosher (like fruits and vegetables); not kosher but with the potential to be made so by special processing; or not kosher—without the possibility of ever becoming kosher (like pork and shellfish).

What Makes It Kosher?

Kosher wines are produced under the strict supervision of a rabbi. To qualify as kosher, certain regulations have to be followed. Because the Holy Land has such a sanctified status in Judaism, some practices are mandated for wineries in Israel but not for those outside of Israel. Qualifying for kosher status extends from the vineyard to the table:

- The vines have to be at least four years old before the grapes can be made into wine. (In Israel, this applies both to grapes grown in one's own vineyard and to grapes purchased from another source.)
- For wineries in Israel, the vineyard must be left fallow every seventh year, and the growing of other fruits or vegetables in the vineyard is prohibited.
- Only Sabbath observant workers are allowed to take part in making the wine. Even after the wine has gone into barrels and been given a rabbinical seal, a *shomer*—or watchman—has to guard it. And no work can be performed on a holy day.
- All the equipment, tools, materials, and storage facilities may be used solely for making kosher products.
- No animal products may be used to produce kosher wine. Instead of using gelatin or egg whites in the fining process, non-animal fining agents (such as bentonite clay) or kosher fish gelatin are used.
- No leavens are permitted. While yeasts are part of winemaking, they must be certified kosher.

In Israel, 1 percent of the finished wine has to be discarded. This practice commemorates the time before the Roman conquest when tithing was mandatory.

There's Kosher, and Then There's Kosher!

For observant Jewish people, kosher wine is holy in nature. And to retain its "kosherness," it must be opened and poured by equally observant Jewish individuals.

In answer to the social and economic limitations this poses—to restaurants, for example—there is *mevushal* wine. It undergoes an additional process to retain its religious purity no matter who opens and pours it. In a sense it's super-kosher.

Through the Grapevine

but is it certified?

A wine's label tells you if a wine is kosher. You'll see an *O* with a *U* inside of it with a *P* near it—a sign that the world's largest kosher certification organization has approved it. A wine label that reads "Made from grapes that are not *orlah*" indicates that the winery observed the age rule—that the vines were at least four years old.

Mevushal means "boiled." In reality, the wine isn't boiled; it's subjected to flash pasteurization. Wines are pasteurized by heating them to about 185°F for one minute—or flash pasteurized by heating them to 203°F for a few seconds—followed by rapid cooling.

Kosher Kudos

In the United States, the largest producer and importer of kosher wine is the Herzog family, whose labels include Baron Herzog, Herzog Wine Cellars, and Weinstock Cellars. In Europe, a number of well-known wineries have set aside a portion of their production for kosher wines. And in Israel, a new generation of wine-makers is producing outstanding wines. Here are just a few of the high-quality kosher wine producers:

- Hagafen Cellars: *California*
- Gan Eden Winery: *California*
- Château Sarget de Gruaud Larose: *France*

- Barkan: *Israel*
- Gamla: *Israel*
- Bartenura: *Italy*
- Ramon Cardova: *Spain*
- Hafner Koscher Wein: *Austria*
- Backsberg: *South Africa*
- Teal Lake: *Australia*
- Alfasi: *Chile*

Through the Grapevine

would louis approve?

Pasteurization changes a wine's characteristics to some degree. Some winemakers say it actually enhances a wine's flavor. For non-kosher wines, pasteurization is done to kill bacteria (which includes bacteria necessary for aging) and is primarily used for ordinary, less expensive wines that are meant for early consumption.

PLOWING THE GOOD EARTH

It was only a matter of time before the organic movement reached the vineyards. Most winemakers are farmers. The wines they produce will be only as good as the grapes they grow. So they have a natural interest in growing the best-tasting fruit and maintaining the health of the land for years to come.

Conventional vs. Organic Farming

All grape growers face the same natural obstacles: weather, pests, disease, weeds. Conventional techniques adopted over the last fifty years to meet nature's challenges have come from man's own inventions—insecticides, chemical fertilizers, fumigants, and herbicides.

Organic farming forsakes chemicals in favor of more "natural" techniques. From a practical viewpoint this means that organic farmers will:

- Fertilize using composted animal manure or algae.
- Combat weeds by mowing them periodically and allowing them to rot back into the ground, providing organic fertilizer.
- Get rid of insects by growing other plants in the vineyard to attract "beneficial" bugs to act as predators.

Organic farming is as much philosophy as practice. The objective is balance in nature and the long-term health of the soil, the plants and, ultimately, the wine drinker. Grapes grown in this fashion can be government certified as organic grapes. The wine can then be advertised as wine from "organically grown grapes."

The irony is that many producers are using organic techniques because they make good sense—but not seeking certification because of the rigidity of government oversight.

Conventional vs. Organic Winemaking

The term *organic*—or, more precisely, the government certification of a wine as "organic"—doesn't stop at the harvest. Organic winemakers have to use only approved organic methods in cellar operations as well. The subject of "organic" has been muddied over the practice of adding sulfur dioxide (sulfites), which is the main ingredient wineries use to extend the shelf life of wine.

The health effects of sulfites are negligible except for a small percentage of people who are particularly sensitive to them. It's difficult to make a wine that will keep for any length of time without adding at least some sulfites to those that are naturally produced by the yeasts during fermentation. But to be able to call a wine "organic," the winemaker has to abide by strict, government-mandated sulfite rules.

Is It the Real Deal?

Organic claims on store shelves are just plain confusing. When you want an organic alternative to conventional wine, who and what should you believe? The answer is on the label—if you understand what the terms mean. There are four categories that organic wines can claim:

- **100% Organic**. The wine must be from 100 percent organically produced ingredients. There can be no added sulfites. It can have naturally occurring sulfites from fermentation, but they have to measure less than 100 parts per million.
- **Organic.** The wine must be from 95 percent organic ingredients. The non-organic 5 percent has to be either an agricultural ingredient that's not organically available or another substance like added yeast. There can be no added sulfites, but naturally occurring sulfites can measure up to 100 parts per million.
- **Made with Organic Ingredients/Organic Grapes/Organically Grown Grapes.** The wine must be from 70 percent organic ingredients. Sulfites have to measure below 100 parts per million.
- **Some Organic Ingredients.** The wine has less than 70 percent organic ingredients. The label can't have any information about a certifying agency or any other reference to organic content.

Simply put, "organic" wines are made from certified organic grapes and contain no additives such as sulfites. Wineries that use organic grapes but add sulfites or other additives can only be labeled "made with organically grown grapes."

To give you a leg up on your next organic wine-buying expedition, here are some wineries that produce certified organic wines:

- Frey Vineyards: *California*
- Badger Mountain Vineyard: *Washington*
- Bonterra Vineyards: *California*
- Cooper Mountain Vineyards: *Oregon*
- Organic Wine Works: *California*

Through the Grapevine

check the fine print

Often, kosher wines may be the answer for vegans—but not always. Kosher gelatin, sometimes used as the fining agent, can be made with fish bones and the skins of beef. Because the product is not real flesh and has undergone significant changes to make it kosher, it's considered not to be meat.

THE VEGETARIAN AND VEGAN CONUNDRUM

Vegetarians and vegans adhere to a diet of vegetables, fruits, grains, and nuts. While vegetarians limit their intake of animal product—sometimes making exceptions for milk and cheese—vegans eliminate animal products altogether. Winemakers—both organic and non-organic—often use animal-based products in the fining process to clarify the wine. The fining agents act as magnets to attract the unwanted material, then fall to the bottom of the tank. The clear wine is siphoned off, but trace amounts of the fining agent may linger in the finished wine. Wines suitable for vegans use earth-based fining agents such as bentonite clay, diatomaceous earth, carbon, and kaolin (similar to bentonite). But the fining agents aren't listed on the label, and you have to do some investigating. It's not that vegan wines are scarce. There are lots of them. They're just not advertised as vegan.

A word to the wise vegan: A suitable wine in one vintage may not be suitable in the next. Winemakers can change their fining agents from one year to the next. You might have to make a call to the producer or exporter to find out. A simpler solution to finding a vegan-friendly wine is to look for "unfined" wines. And that's what it will say on the label.

Filtering is another process to remove impurities. A wine can be both fined and filtered, it can undergo one process without the other, or it can undergo neither. "Unfined" on the label means that no clarifying agent has been used.

chapter 3

WHAT'$ NEW IN THE "OLD WORLD"

· · · · · · · · · · · · · · · ·

In winespeak, Europe and the rest of the Mediterranean basin are called the "Old World"—because it was there that the grapevines were first so widely established. The Old World is more than a geographical area. It's a tradition. Old World winemakers have always favored *terroir* ("the soil") over technique. It's the sense that the earth, the sun, and the climate should have (and do have) more influence on the nature of the wine than the winemaker. Let's review the Old World wine regions and the wines they produce.

· · · · · · · · · · · · · · · ·

MR. CHEAP

FRANCE

As Julius Caesar concluded 2,000 years ago, France proved a pretty good place to grow wine grapes. Through trial and error, and centuries of careful cultivation and meticulous recordkeeping, the French learned how to make excellent wine. Many people—particularly the French—would say they defined, and set the standards for superior wine. Even when their grape varietals have been transplanted half-way around the world, others tend to retain their original French names: Cabernet Sauvignon, Cabernet Franc, Sauvignon Blanc, and Pinot Noir, for example.

It's generally accepted that France produces many "best of" types in the following categories:

- Their champagnes are considered the best sparkling wines.
- Their Alsace region produces the ultimate Gewürztraminer.
- Their Pauillac and Margaux districts of Bordeaux produce the finest Cabernet Sauvignon–based wines.
- Their Bordeaux regions of Saint-Emilion and Pomerol are known for their superior Merlot.
- The grand cru vineyards of the Côte de Beaune produce the finest Chardonnays.
- Some of the most refined Sauvignon Blanc–based wines come from Sancerre.
- Chenin Blanc is in its glory along the Loire River.
- Sauternes is widely acclaimed as the world's finest dessert wine.
- The prototype of Pinot Noir comes from the vineyards of Côte de Nuits in Burgundy.

And there's plenty to brag about from France's other regions as well. Because some of the regions are not so high profile, they often offer real bargains for wine lovers.

Reading French Wine Labels

In order to understand the degrees of specificity of French wine labeling, think of an archery target. The outer circle is all of France. The next-largest circle is a region of France, such as Bordeaux. The next circle in is a district—Médoc, for example. Within that circle is the commune—say, Pauillac. Finally, the bull's-eye: the individual producer—a château or domaine. The better—and usually more expensive—the wine, the more specific is the indicated source of the wine.

The French are très concerned about the quality of their wines. So they created a system for regulating the quality and ranking the wines. The rankings appear on the labels, as follows:

- **Appellation d'Origine Contrôlée (AOC or AC)**—the most widely applied standard used on French wine labels. It indicates that the wine meets the rigorous legal standards for the area indicated: the more specific the area of origin, the higher the standards.

- **Vins Délimité de Qualité Supérieure (VDQS)**—a second set of standards for wines in areas not covered by AOC law. Although a notch down in quality, VDQS is still a reliable government guarantee of quality.
- **Vin de pays**—a third, and slightly more relaxed set of rules that regulate "country" wines. The phrase is always followed by a place name—be it larger (region) or smaller (community).
- **Vin de table or vin ordinaire**—"table" wines whose place names are "France." This is the lowest category of wine in the French system.

Within France, each region has its own system of organization and classification. And each region is known for producing specific wines.

Bordeaux

Bordeaux, an industrial city in southwestern France, is the center of the world's most famous wine region. The types of wine produced there include:

- **Dry white wines**—blends of Sauvignon Blanc and Sémillon.
- **Sweet dessert wines**—blends of Sauvignon Blanc, Sémillon, and Muscadelle afflicted with *Botrytis cinerea* (noble rot).
- **Medium-bodied red wines**—blends of Cabernet Sauvignon, Merlot, Cabernet Franc, Malbec, and Petit Verdot. (Some subregions produce wine made primarily from Cabernet, while Merlot is the dominant grape in other areas.)

The most important subregions of Bordeaux are Sauternes (famous for its dessert wines), Pomerol (known for Merlot-dominant reds), Saint-Emilion (more Merlot-based reds), Entre-Deux-Mers (light whites), Graves (home of both fine dry whites and Cabernet-based reds), and Médoc (Cabernet-based reds). Médoc is probably the most famous of the Bordeaux subregions and has communes within its borders that also qualify for village appellation status: Saint-Estephe, Saint-Julien, Margaux, Pauillac, Listrac, and Moulis.

Premier Cru Wines

Back in 1855, Napoleon III went to the wine brokers of Bordeaux and asked them to rate the red wines of Médoc. This they did by looking at the price history of the wines—the operating theory being that the most expensive wines would be the best. The brokers came up with the sixty-one "best" wine estates in Médoc and then ranked them one through five—with one being the highest rank. This classification is called *premier cru* (meaning "first growth").

The four châteaus that were first awarded this classification are Lafite Rothschild, Latour, Margaux, and Haut-Brion. In 1973, Château Mouton-Rothschild was upgraded to premier cru status. You'll see "Premier Grand Cru Classé" on their labels.

With a total of only sixty-one châteaus listed in the original classification, thousands of other producers in Médoc were left out. In 1932, another classification, *cru bourgeois*, was created to include the best of them.

Burgundy

In Bordeaux, the wine estates are called châteaus. In Burgundy, they're called domaines. That's just your first clue that the two regions are figuratively (and geographically) miles apart. While large producers dominate in Bordeaux, the Burgundy region has thousands of small growers who often own only very small pieces of vineyard land. And one vineyard can be divided up into dozens of owners.

However, Burgundy is pretty predictable when it comes to how they construct their wines. Red wines are made from the Pinot Noir grape. White wines are made from Chardonnay. And Beaujolais, in the southern part of the region, makes light and fruity reds from the Gamay grape.

Traveling from north to south through the heart of France, you pass through the subregions of Burgundy in sequence:

- **Chablis**—known for its dry white wines
- **Côte de Nuits**—home of the most noteworthy reds
- **Côte de Beaune**—producer of both reds and whites, but known especially for great whites
- **Côte Chalonnaise**—regarded as a lesser region but still home to good reds and whites
- **Mâcon**—known for whites that offer excellent values
- **Beaujolais**—home to Gamay production

the cat's meow

Premier cru is top dog in Bordeaux . . . but *grand cru* ("great growth") is the cat's meow in Burgundy. The designation is reserved for specific vineyards that, based on their location and long-term track record, produce the best wines. The labels will bear only the name of the vineyard—not the name of any village.

Role of Négociants

Négociant is French for "merchant" or "dealer." Traditionally, *négociants* bought wines, blended and bottled them, and shipped them. They could take wines from small producers and market them on a more commercially viable scale. More recently, their roles have expanded to buying grapes and making wine. They represent wines of all quality levels—including grand cru.

Large *négociant* houses blend wines to produce unique house styles. Some of these well-known houses include Louis Jadot, Joseph Drouhin, Georges Duboeuf, and Louis Latour.

$OMMELIER CENTS

the slope of gold

Côte de Nuits and Côte de Beaune, together, are known as the Côte d'Or—the "slope of gold." The area has a lot of grand cru and premier cru vineyards that produce some of Burgundy's most famous and most expensive wines, including Corton-Charlemagne, Montrachet, Romanée-Conti, Chambertin, Bonnes Mares, and Clos de Vougeot. These wines will set you back quite a few dollars, so wait for major markdowns!

Rhone

Continuing south from Burgundy, you enter the Rhone Valley—home to earthy, gutsy wines, both red and white. The northern and southern regions are distinctly different in terms of their wines. Northern reds are Syrah-based and worthy of aging. You'll run into names like Côte Rôtie, Hermitage, Crozes-Hermitage, Cornas, and St. Joseph. The whites are made from Viognier (like Condrieu) or a blend of Marsanne and Roussane (like Hermitage).

Most Rhone wines come from the south—in the form of Côtes du Rhone. The primary grape variety is Grenache. Southern Rhone is also famous for its Châteauneuf-du-Pape, which can be made with as many as thirteen grape varieties—both red and white (although Grenache, Mourvèdre, and Syrah predominate).

Southwest of Châteauneuf-du-Pape is Tavel, where they produce France's best-known and most distinguished Rosés. They're dry and full-bodied and have an international reputation.

Loire

The Loire Valley stretches across northwest France, following the Loire River. The area has a reputation for its non-Chardonnay white wines. The most important ones include:

- **Muscadet**—a light, dry wine that (unlike most other French wines) is named after the grape variety
- **Vouvray**—made from the Chenin Blanc grape into wines that can range from bone dry to off-dry to sparkling
- **Pouilly-Fumé**—straight Sauvignon Blanc made in a rich style

- **Sancerre**—unblended Sauvignon Blanc in a lighter, drier, livelier style than the Pouilly-Fumé

It's easy to confuse the names Pouilly-Fumé and Pouilly-Fuissé, but they're two different wines from two entirely different areas in France. Pouilly-Fuissé is a Chardonnay from the Mâcon region of Burgundy and is a much more full-bodied wine.

Through the Grapevine

papa's home!

Châteuneuf-du-Pape means "new home of the pope." It dates back to the fourteenth century when the papal court was relocated to nearby Avignon and a summer palace was built in a village just north of the city (now known as Châteauneuf-du-Pape).

Alsace

Historically, Alsace (the area across the Rhine River from Germany) has belonged to whoever won the most recent war between France and Germany. Since World War I, it's been a part of France. Because of its background, Alsace has much in common with Germany. Both Alsace and Germany grow the same grapes—although the wines of Alsace are generally drier than those of Germany. And, contrary to the rest of France, Alsace labels its wines with the varietal name. Regulations in Alsace require that a wine carrying a varietal name contain 100 percent of that grape. The most important varietals are:

- Riesling
- Muscat

- Gewürztraminer
- Sylvaner
- Pinot Gris

A small amount of Pinot Noir (the only grape permitted for red wine) is grown in Alsace and is often used for Rosé wines.

ITALY

Italy produces—and drinks—more wine than any other country. Yes, the citizens of little Italy drink more wine than anyone. An area like Bordeaux may have well over 12,000 producers, but Italy has 1.2 million growers! And on the consumption side, Italians drink twenty-six gallons per person each year—compared to just three gallons for Americans. Let's just say, the Italians love their vino, and for good reason.

$OMMELIER CENTS

italian style
Italy makes more than 2,000 kinds of wine within its borders. Everywhere you go in Italy, you see grapevines growing. And the grapes are overwhelmingly Italian: Nebbiolo, Sangiovese, Barbera, Dolcetto. In this case, variety is the spice of life! Sample Italian wines widely, as many are delicious and affordable.

Don't expect to find the grape names on the labels . . . except sometimes. For the most part, Italians name their wines after places—just like the French do. Take Chianti Classico as an example. It's made primarily from the Sangiovese grape, but the wine is named after the Chianti Classico winemaking district. Then there's

Barbera. It's the name of a grape. In the town of Asti, they name their wine Barbera d'Asti. In Alba, they call it Barbera d'Alba. All right, that seems simple enough. But not all Barbera wines use the grape name on the label.

In 1963, Italy developed a system—modeled after the French one—to control the quality of their wines and classify them. The regulations govern yields, grapes that can be used for specific wines, viticulture practices, and alcohol levels. From top to bottom, the categories are:

- **Denominazione di Origine Controllata e Garantita (DOCG)**—Meaning "Controlled and Guaranteed Denomination of Origin," it's the highest category of wine and indicates that the quality is not only "controlled"—it's "guaranteed" by the government.
- **Denominazione di Origine Controllata (DOC)**—The wines must meet certain standards and come from specific geographic areas.
- **Vino da tavola**—Italy's "table wine" category, it indicates a simple, everyday wine.

It's important to remember that DOC/DOCG status is a guarantee of where and how the wine is produced. It's not a guarantee of how it will taste. Some of the "best" and priciest wines from Italy don't have DOC status.

In the 1970s, a group of winemakers in Tuscany ran afoul of the DOC regulations by using disallowed grape varieties—like Cabernet Sauvignon and Merlot—in addition to the native Sangiovese or by producing 100 percent Sangiovese wines. The wines turned out to be terrific and much sought-after, but (because they were against the law) they were labeled "vino da tavola." They skyrocketed in price anyway. They're known as "Super Tuscans."

Since then, a new official quality category has been created whose rules are less strict than those of the DOC. It's called *IGT* (Indicazione Geografica Tipica). Some of the esteemed Super Tuscans were thus upgraded to IGT status.

Italy's Wine Regions

Italy has twenty wine regions that are geographically identical to its political regions. The regions in the north are the most recognized, but southern Italy—viticulture areas such as Campania, Umbria, Basilicata, and the islands of Sicily and Sardinia—are making huge inroads in producing wines of quality and marketability. Unique indigenous varieties—like Fiano di Avellino from Campania and Vermentino from Sardinia—have really taken off.

$OMMELIER CENTS

preemie find
Rosso di Montalcino is made from the same Brunello grape in the same area of Montalcino. The difference is that it only has to age for one year before its release. It's lighter, less intense . . . and cheaper.

In the north, the regions of Piedmont, Tuscany, and Veneto are the most familiar. Piedmont (meaning "foot of the mountain") in the northwest lies at the base of the Alps. Nebbiolo reigns, producing the famous Barolo and Barbaresco—two robust reds. They're very similar to each other, but Barolo is fuller-bodied and needs more aging. (Barolo is sometimes referred to as the "king" of Italian wines.) Other popular reds include Barbera, Dolcetto, and Bonardo. Among the whites are the Muscat-based Asti Spumante and Moscato d'Asti and the dry white Gavi from the Cortese grape.

Tuscany, with its enchanted landscapes and historic castles, is responsible for the world-famous Chianti—whose production goes back centuries. Much more recent is Brunello di Montalcino, made in an area south of Chianti from a Sangiovese clone. It's big, tannic, and powerful and has one of the longest aging requirements (four years) in Italy.

Another Tuscan favorite is Vino Nobile di Montepulciano from 60 percent to 80 percent Sangiovese. Tuscany's most important white grape is Trebbiano.

Veneto in the northeast is the third largest region in terms of production and serves up some of the more familiar Italian exports: Soave, the sparkling Prosecco, and Valpolicella. While Valpolicella is rather light and fruity, another version—Amarone della Valpolicella—is rich, high in alcohol (14 to 16 percent), and long-lived.

Known simply as Amarone, the wine is made from grapes that have been dried on mats for several months before fermentation, concentrating the sugars and flavors.

And what about the ubiquitous Pinot Grigio, the number one imported table wine in the United States? Probably the best ones come from the two northeastern-most regions of Alto Adige (which borders Austria) and Fruili (bordering Slovenia).

GERMANY

Talk about intimidating! Other than natives, who can read a German wine label? If they want you to drink their wines, you'd think they would make buying one easier. Actually, they're trying.

In the German quality rating system, the highest quality wines are labeled QmP (Qualitätswein mit Prä-dikat), meaning "quality wine with distinction." QmP wines (the ones primarily exported) are categorized by the ripeness of the grapes when they're harvested. Because Germany's vineyards are so far north, it's difficult to get the grapes to ripen. Hence, grape sugars are highly prized. The riper the grape, the higher the sugar content—and, in Germany's opinion, the higher the quality of the wine. From the least ripe (lowest) to the ripest (highest) are:

- Kabinett
- Spätlese
- Auslese
- Beerenauslese
- Trockenbeerenauslese
- Eiswein

At the two lower levels, the grapes can be fermented to produce a completely dry wine. So, a rule-of-thumb for choosing a dry German wine is to look for Kabinett on the label. At the highest ripeness levels, the grapes have so much sugar at harvest that the wines can't help but be sweet.

Some wine drinkers equate German wines with sweetness. In today's environment of "dry is better," German producers are trying to make it easier for consumers to identify their dry wines. Words to look for if you're trying to find a dry style:

- **Trocken.** It means dry; *halbtrocken* is "half dry."
- **Classic.** It indicates a dry, uncomplicated varietal. The term will appear next to the grape name.
- **Selection.** In addition to being dry, these are premium varietals that have to come from an individual vineyard named on the label. The term will appear after the vineyard site.

When all is said and done, it's really Germany's sweet wines that take the prizes. The late harvest wines from grapes picked long into the fall, the botricized grapes whose sweetness comes from noble rot, and the ice wines whose grapes were left to freeze on the vines: They're internationally acclaimed.

Germany's Wine Regions

With the exception of a couple of regions in the east, most of Germany's wine regions are concentrated in the south and southwestern part of the country. They are among the most northerly wine regions in the world. Germany's most famous winemaking areas are the Mosel-Saar-Ruwer region (along the Mosel River and its two tributaries) and the three contiguous regions along the Rhine River—Rheingau, Rheinhessen, and Pfalz.

With Germany's climate, 85 percent of the country's wines are white—because red grapes don't ripen well under cool conditions. The wines they produce are relatively low in alcohol. Riesling is Germany's signature grape. But other varieties are more widely planted. Müller-Thurgau, a cross between Riesling and Sylvaner, ripens earlier than Riesling and takes the anxiety out of harvesting. However, the grapes don't reach the same heights of great wine as Riesling.

Through the Grapevine

so, what's with the different color bottles?

The color of the tall, slender bottles tells you what region the wine comes from. Brown bottles come from the Rhine region. Green bottles come from the Mosel area or from Alsace. The shape is used elsewhere around the world for wines made from grape varieties associated with Germany—like Riesling and Gewürztraminer.

German Wine Labels

German labels can contain both a varietal and a geographic location. In the German language, adding *er* at the end of a noun makes it possessive. On wine labels, *er* is added to the name of the town or village where the wine was made. The name of the town in the possessive form is followed by the name of the specific vineyard. So, a label that reads "Niersteiner Oelberg Riesling Spätlese" tells you that the name of the town is Nierstein, the vineyard (in the town of Nierstein) is Oelberg, the varietal is Riesling, and the ripeness level is Spätlese.

SPAIN

There was a time not too long ago that Spain was known for producing inexpensive and unremarkable reds. Well, times have changed—due, in part, to regulations (similar to those in France) that were adopted to improve the quality of the wines. On top of that, Spanish winemakers adopted modern production methods and expanded into new regions. All had a positive effect on Spain's wines. Spain's rating system from highest quality to lowest is:

- **Denominación de Origen Calificaca (DOCa)**—meaning "qualified designation of origin."
- **Denominación de Origen (DO)**—meaning "designation of origin."
- **Vino de la tierra**—a table wine category the equivalent of France's vins de pays.

Rioja

Rioja, Spain's oldest and most famous wine region, became the first DO when the system was set up in 1926. And when the system was refined in 1991, Rioja became the first region to be promoted to DOCa status. Tempranillo is king in Rioja. Other grapes—Garnacha, Graciano, and Mazuelo—are used for blending, but Tempranillo takes center stage.

The wines range from delicate to big and alcoholic. The traditional method of production included significant aging in oak barrels. Reds that are aged for two years are labeled *crianza*. After three years of aging, they become *riserva*. And five years or more makes them *gran reserva*. Because the oak dominated the fruit flavors in an era when international wine drinkers preferred fruit, winemakers have begun replacing some of the barrel aging with bottle aging.

Other Spanish Winemaking Regions

Spain has more vineyard acreage than any other country in the world. And regions other than Rioja are making names for themselves. Ribera del Duero, north of Madrid, is a relatively new "official" wine region, having been designated a DO in 1982. For the hundred plus years preceding that, wine production was dominated by one estate—Vega Sicilia. Today, wineries are springing up all over. Some of the more prominent include:

- Penedés, Navarra, Rueda, and Rías Biaxas in Galicia are all coming into their own.
- Penedés is home to most of the Cava-producing (sparkling wine) wineries, which account for one-fifth of the vineyards. The companies also make still wines—mostly whites from the Xarel-lo, Macabeo, and Parellada grapes.

- Navarra used to offer easy-drinking Rosés but has traded them in for red wines from Tempranillo, Cabernet Sauvignon, and Merlot.
- Rueda has become famous for producing fresh and fruity white wines from the Verdejo grape—sometimes blended with Sauvignon Blanc.
- Rías Baixas is producing the much-acclaimed Albariño—the rich and complex white with high levels of acidity and alcohol.

PORTUGAL

Portugal may be better known for Port and Madeira, but it's no newcomer to making table wines. Vineyards have flourished for centuries, and records show wine exports dating back to 1367. Portugal has an appellations system similar to other Old World countries, but it seems to be less important as a new generation of winemakers has produced wines with proprietary names not tied to regional dictates.

One of Portugal's notable exports is Vinho Verde. It's both a red and a white, but you're likely to see only the white. The reds are consumed mostly within Portugal's borders. Vinho Verde, which is the name of the appellation, means "green wine." It's so named because the grapes are picked early and the wine is drunk young. Its slight effervescence also qualifies it as a semi-sparkling wine. The better versions are made from the Alvarinho grape—the same one that makes Spain's Albariño wine. The Spanish and Portuguese districts are just across the border from each other.

Portugal is becoming a wonderful source for dry reds—particularly from the Douro and Dão regions.

Barca Velha from Douro is a highly sought-after—and expensive—red that's made only in the better vintages. It's intense and full-bodied and needs time to age.

AUSTRIA

Austria has perhaps the most stringent wine production and labeling regulations anywhere—the result of a scandal in 1985. Because sweet, late harvest wines are so prized and expensive, a small group of unscrupulous producers adulterated ordinary wines with diethylene glycol (a substance related to antifreeze) to sweeten them. They labeled them late harvest and tried to pass them off as the real thing. The affair caused Austrian wine exports to plummet within the year to less than one-fifth of what they had been sending to other countries. The government stepped in, and new regulations were implemented to keep anything similar from happening again. Today, Austria is successfully exporting more of its wines than ever—dry whites in addition to the late harvest wines.

Through the Grapevine

lemberger, anyone?

No, not the cheese. That's Limburger. Lemberger is a little-known German grape variety (*Blaufränkisch* in German) that's also grown in Austria. It makes a fruity but dry red. The wines are typically light-bodied—not unlike Beaujolais.

You might expect that Austria would produce wines more like its neighbor, Germany. But the Austrian style is dry—more like Alsace. Austria's most famous grape is Grüner Veltliner—a longtime favorite with Austrians and now making a big splash around the world. It produces wines that are typically dry, medium-bodied, and spicy. Austrian wines also rely on Riesling, Gewürztraminer, and Weissburgunder (Pinot Blanc). Reds, usually more difficult to find, are typically light.

Much like the German system of rating quality on sweetness, the quality levels are (in ascending order): Spätlese, Auslese, Ausbruch, and Trockenbeerenauslese.

chapter 4

WHAT'$ NEW IN THE "NEW WORLD"

. . . .

"New World" was at one time a less-than-flattering term for the upstart winemakers outside of Europe. Since then, many of the philosophical borders between the "Old World" and the "New World" have eroded as "Old World" countries adapt to technological innovation and "New World" winemakers increasingly adopt traditional techniques. In winemaking, though, the effect of the land on the final product is paramount. And geography will always separate the two worlds.

. . . .

MR. CHEAP'

AUSTRALIA

For a country widely known for its beer-drinking aficionados, Australia sure has made a name for itself in the wine world. In fact, Australia has become the biggest wine exporter after Italy, France, and Spain. What makes it such an awesome feat is that 75 percent of Australia's land can't support agriculture of any kind. There are no native vines in Australia. And it was really European immigration to Australia that helped shape the wine industry.

The Chain Gang

Beginning in 1788, England shipped off its felons to Australia—to exile them and to provide labor to create an infrastructure there. The "relocation" stopped in the middle of the nineteenth century when there were enough people to do the work.

The state of South Australia was the only "free" state—meaning that it was the only area not settled by British convicts. In 1836, the land was awarded to George Fife Angus, founder of the South Australian Company. He needed settlers to help develop the land, and he began to recruit them. It was ideal timing for European Lutherans who were fleeing the Continent because of religious persecution. They could buy land in South Australia for very little money in return for farming the land.

Many of the new immigrants came from Germany and left their imprint in town names, traditional foods—and wines. The area is still renowned for its Rieslings. By the 1890s, the Barossa, Hunter, and Yarra Valleys were all producing wine.

why cheap wines are so darn good

Kudos to the Australian winemakers who blanketed the market with inexpensive wines that tasted very good for the price—ripe, fruity, and delicious. Their wines caught on quickly in England and America, which motivated emerging "New World" countries like Chile and Argentina to beef up their production of well-made affordable wines. Wineries in traditional "Old World" nations—France, Spain, Italy, and Germany—didn't want to see their market shares dwindle so modernized their facilities to streamline and improve the quality of their more basic wines.

Awesome Aussie Wines

Prior to the 1950s, wine production in Australia focused on fortified wines. They were the most affordable wines during the worldwide Depression, and the added alcohol made them better for longer storage. The 1960s and 1970s saw a shift toward table wines—first the sweeter versions and, ultimately, dry styles.

While there's amazing diversity in Australian wines, they could be described as fun, bold, and affordable. Winemakers have been creative in their blends of Chardonnay-Sémillon and Shiraz-Cabernet. Probably the country's best reds are blends of Shiraz—recently with Viogner and other Rhone varieties as well as with Cabernet. Shiraz—the Aussie name for Syrah—is Australia's utility grape. It can be made lots of ways—big and oaky to go with a well-aged steak or light enough for summer sipping. Australia has been so successful in marketing their Shiraz wines that other countries have recently chosen to label their Syrah "Shiraz."

You can find some true treasures in Australia's dessert wines—nicknamed "stickies." Also of local interest is sparkling Shiraz—dark, dry, and slightly fizzy.

Australia's Wine Regions

Like the United States, Australia has a number of outstanding wine regions—fifty regions and subregions spread throughout the country. Many of them are clustered in southeastern Australia—particularly in the states of South Australia, Victoria, and New South Wales—and the more isolated maritime area of Western Australia. Some of Australia's prominent regions include:

- **Barossa Valley in South Australia**—This area is home to some of Australia's most famous wineries. Known for Riesling, Shiraz, and Cabernet Sauvignon.
- **Coonawara in South Australia**—This region is noted for its reddish-colored "terra rossa" soil. Popular wines are Shiraz and Cabernet Sauvignon.

- **Yarra Valley in Victoria**—This region is known especially for Pinot Noir and Cabernet Sauvignon.
- **Hunter Valley in New South Wales**—This region of Australia produces Sémillon and Cabernet Sauvignon among many others.

In addition to Cabernet, Shiraz, Pinot Noir, Riesling, and Sémillon (pronounced SEH-meh-lon) Down Under, Australian wines include Merlot, Grenache, Chardonnay, and Sauvignon Blanc.

NEW ZEALAND

All was quiet on the New Zealand wine front when—BOOM—suddenly the country started garnering prestigious wine awards. Who, outside of New Zealanders, even knew that grapes were growing there? Grapevines were first planted on New Zealand's North Island in 1816, but not much of note happened after that—until the 1980s.

In 1986, New Zealand took "best wine" medals three days in a row in international competition. The winning wine was a Sauvignon Blanc from the Marlborough region—and wine drinkers took notice. Sauvignon Blanc has become something of the country's goodwill ambassador to the rest of the world, but its other wines have as much to offer.

A Land of Distinction

New Zealand has the distinction of having the most easterly vineyards—being closest to the International Date Line—and the world's most southern vineyards. The country's winemaking regions are located on the two large islands that comprise most of New Zealand. The warmer North Island has climatic differences from the cooler South Island, but both benefit from the cool ocean breezes. No location in New Zealand is farther than seventy-five miles from the water.

The emphasis is on growing grapes that suit cool growing conditions—mostly Chardonnay, Sauvignon Blanc, and Pinot Noir. These varieties make up 60 percent of the country's total vineyard area.

Through the Grapevine

a nose for whites

New Zealand producers are turning their attention to another category of wines: aromatic whites—primarily Riesling but also Pinot Gris, Gewürztraminer, and Sémillon. They're all over the board in terms of sweetness levels. And there's usually no indication on the label to tell you.

Regions and their Wines

The cultivated areas of New Zealand span 720 miles from north to south, and—except for the most southerly region—they all are on the eastern coastline. The development of vineyard land has roughly corresponded to population growth, which, in the twentieth century, started in the area around Auckland.

North Island

Auckland has a third of the country's population. While it produces its own wines, it's also a center of wine commerce where wines from other regions are vinified and blended. Gisborne produces over a third of the country's wine—most of it bulk wine. But it also has a reputation for fine wines and has been called the Chardonnay capital of New Zealand.

Hawke's Bay is one of New Zealand's older and best wine regions and often records the most sunshine hours. Chardonnay and Cabernet Sauvignon have been the most important varietals. Wellington is known for outstanding Pinot Noirs.

South Island

Marlborough's first vineyards were planted in 1973. And by 1990, the region had become the largest vine-growing area with 40 percent of the country's total vineyards. Sauvignon Blanc is the most popular varietal, with Chardonnay second. Riesling is grown too—and, increasingly, Pinot Noir. Otago is the most southerly region where the vineyards are planted in hillside locations to minimize the danger of frost. The area is particularly known for its Pinot Noir and Gewürztraminer.

$OMMELIER CENTS

new zealand options

According to *www.foodandwine.com*, although more widely known for their Sauvignon Blancs, New Zealand's very affordable 2002 Spy Valley Gewürztraminer, with its quite different Kiwi-grown grape, delivered an intense Alsace-style white. Ask your favorite retailer to recommend other tasty, affordable treats from New Zealand.

New Zealand Winemakers

One way New Zealand wines came so far so fast is that its young winemakers traveled to Europe during the Northern Hemisphere's harvest season to gain experience in the world's classic wine regions. What they learned they put into practice back home.

Without a long winemaking tradition in their own country, New Zealand winemakers are free to express their own styles—and they do.

SOUTH AFRICA

Most of South Africa's vineyards are clustered in the southwest in an area near the Cape of Good Hope that's become known as Cape Winelands. It has a Mediterranean climate—warm, dry summers and rainfall during the mild winter months. Perfect for growing grapes.

> **$OMMELIER CENTS**
>
> **south african roots**
> Winemaking goes back to the early Dutch settlers. In fact, it was the Dutch governor who, in 1655, planted the first vines. Four years later the grapes were pressed into wine. But the French Huguenots—fleeing religious persecution back home—really brought a serious tradition of winemaking to South Africa. Today their traditional "roots" and winemaking skills offer the world market well-made, tasty, and affordable wines.

In the eighteenth century, the Cape established itself on the world wine stage with its Muscat-based dessert wine called Constantia. It was much in demand at all the royal courts of Europe. Napoleon, it's rumored, even ordered it from his exile on St. Helena.

In spite of the wild success of Constantia, the wine industry went into a 200-year decline. In 1918, a large farmers' cooperative (the KWV) was formed to control production and the market. It tended to put private wine producers at a disadvantage in favor of bulk grape growers—hardly a recipe for quality and innovation.

Politics took their toll, too. During the years of apartheid, international trade disappeared as sanctions were implemented.

Democracy Turns the Tide

With apartheid abolished in 1991 and sanctions lifted, the South African wine industry could turn its attention to improving its wines to compete in the world market. It imported better vine cuttings, expanded oak aging to commercial wines, and upgraded vineyard management, among other things.

$OMMELIER CENTS

south africa sizzles

Wine authority Joshua Wesson of *www.bestcellars .com* is hot on South Africa, noting that it's a country that's been making wine for 300 years. The lifting of apartheid and the embargo on South African goods has thankfully opened up a new world of grapes and wine to us all. Wesson particularly likes their Pinotage, which he describes as "a wonderfully berry-like grape unique to South Africa," and their Sauvignon Blancs, both of which are often more affordable than their American or European counterparts.

South Africa has only 1.5 percent of the world's vineyards—ranking sixteenth in area planted. But with its large output, South Africa ranks seventh in production, representing 3 percent of the world's wine.

Chenin Blanc—called *Steen* in South Africa—is the country's most planted variety. It's made in a variety of styles including sparkling, late harvest, and Rosé. Following Chenin Blanc in production are Sultana, Colombard, and Chardonnay. White varieties account for about two-thirds of South Africa's grapes, but 80 percent of new plantings are red varieties.

Cabernet Sauvignon is the most planted red variety, followed by Pinotage and Shiraz.

South Africa's most famous wine regions include:

- **Stellenbosch.** Just east of Cape Town, it's home to many of the country's leading estates.
- **Paarl.** Northwest of Cape Town, it's traditionally a white wine region—but is now concentrating on reds.
- **Constantia.** It's the region closest to Cape Town (and home to the once-great dessert wine) where South Africa's first vineyards were planted.

CHILE

Missionaries traveling with the conquistadors in the mid-1500s brought vine cuttings to Chile from their native Spain to produce wine for sacramental purposes. The wines were mostly rustic renditions of Spanish varietals—Pais and Moscatel. The grapes did so well that by the 1800s, Chilean wines were giving Spanish imports a real run for their money. And that was a problem, at least to the Spanish Crown. The Spanish government levied heavy taxes and imposed severe restrictions on winemaking—all of which took its toll on Chilean vineyards.

Following the wars of independence in the nineteenth century, the newly prosperous upper class of Chileans traveled to Europe, where they developed a fondness for French wines. Cuttings from the great Bordeaux varieties were imported, and the modern era of winemaking in Chile was under way.

Virgin Rootstock

In the second half of the nineteenth century, the phylloxera epidemic wiped out the vineyards of Europe and North America. Because Chile was isolated by natural conditions—the Andes to the east, the Pacific to the west, and barren deserts to the north—it remained free of the disease while the rest of the wine world was decimated.

To this day, Chile remains the only country unaffected by phylloxera. Its vinifera vines are the only ones in the world still growing on their own rootstocks.

Carmenère: The Great Masquerade

Carmenère was an important grape of Bordeaux vineyards. When Chile imported vine cuttings from France, Carmenère was high on the list. Then came the phylloxera epidemic and the massive replanting of all the European vineyards. When Bordeaux was replanted, Carmenère was left out. Why? Compared to Merlot—which it resembled—Carmenère was too fussy. It doesn't flower when the springs are cold and wet. It ripens weeks after Merlot does. And it has lower yields than Merlot. It was an easy decision for French growers: Stick with the Merlot!

The climate in Chile, however, is perfect for Carmenère—so it grew happily for years alongside Merlot. Because they look so much alike, Carmenère lost its identity over the years and came to be called Merlot.

As Chilean wines gained popularity in recent years, more of it made its way into the world market. It didn't go unnoticed that Chilean Merlot tasted somewhat stronger and spicier than Merlots from elsewhere. Then in 1994, it was discovered through DNA testing that the Merlot was actually Carmenère!

$OMMELIER CENTS

critic's choices

A few "New World" wines that wine critic Richard Nalley of *www.foodandwine.com* recommends include:

- Argentina's 2002 Los Cardos Chardonnay
- Chile's 2001 Odfjell Armador Cabernet Sauvignon
- South Africa's 2002 Raats Original Chenin Blanc
- Australia's 2002 Rosemount Shiraz

Politics and Investment

The Chilean wine industry has had its ups and downs, in spite of nearly perfect conditions for growing grapes. In the 1940s, Chilean wines grew in popularity—only to lose ground when the government nationalized many of the wineries and restricted production. Even when government regimes changed, civil war brought further instability to the wine industry—until, in 1980, almost half the country's vineyards were out of production.

With stability restored in the '80s, Chile was able to attract significant investment from companies in France, the United States, Australia, Spain, and Japan. Modern technology and replanted vineyards brought new life to Chilean wines. They became known, almost overnight, as excellent, value-priced varietals—with big plans for the fine-wines category.

Through the Grapevine

75 percent rule

In 1995, under the new appellation system, Chile established the 75 percent rule. Seventy-five percent of the contents of a bottle of wine must come from the exact location, variety, and vintage specified on the label. Twenty-five percent is allowed for blending purposes. "Reserva" wines aren't as tightly controlled, and are required only to indicate a place of origin on the label.

Varietals

While Pais and Moscatel are still being turned into wine for the domestic market, the wine industry has invested heavily in high-quality reds for export. Cabernet Sauvignon, Merlot, Pinot Noir, Syrah—and, of course, Carmenère—are the focus. White varietals include Chardonnay, Sauvignon Blanc, Riesling, and Sémillon.

ARGENTINA

Argentina's wines and wine history have always been tied to the country's economic and political circumstances. Spanish settlers first brought "work horse" vines to Argentina as early as the mid-1500s. Criolla (related to Chile's Pais grape) and Cereza were plentiful but didn't make wines of much character. The wines were made with an eye toward ensuring they were able to survive the harrowing shipping conditions to other South American countries.

Two waves of European immigration were responsible for introducing new varieties. In 1816, after Argentina's independence from Spain and again at the turn of the century, settlers from France, Spain, and Italy brought vine cuttings to make the wines they had enjoyed in Europe, including:

- Malbec, Cabernet Sauvignon, Merlot, and Chenin Blanc from France
- Torrontés and Tempranillo from Spain
- Sangiovese, Nebbiolo, Dolcetto, Barbera, and Lambrusco from Italy

---

Through the Grapevine

a leg up

Even though battling desert conditions, Spanish settlers were able to quickly cultivate grape vines because the Huarpe Indians, and the Incans before them, had already established an irrigation system. The new settlers enhanced the system. Relying on the thaw of ice and snow from the Andes Mountains, they created a network of dykes and canals to channel the water to where it was needed.

Quantity vs. Quality

By the 1920s, Argentina had become the eighth richest nation in the world. The Depression set it back, but, under Juan Perón, the country seemed to be recovering. In the mid-1950s, Perón was deposed and a succession of military governments plunged the country into economic and political decline.

With a population that, frankly, drank a lot of wine (twenty-one gallons per capita per year), Argentina's winemakers focused on quantity rather than quality. Massive amounts of rustic "Vino de Mesa" were produced to satisfy domestic demand. In the late '80s and early '90s, Argentina experienced runaway inflation—1,000 percent a year. Price controls were put on wine, forcing some growers to shift to crops other than grapes. For those who continued to grow grapes, a tax policy was established that rewarded the destruction of older vineyards of traditional grape varieties in favor of planting inferior, but high-volume, varieties.

$OMMELIER CENTS

argentina courting favor

Because they are tasty and priced right, wines from Argentina are gaining favor in the U.S. According to *www.looksmart.com*, Bonarda and Malbec blends, as well as pure old-vine Malbec, are often better than similar wines at twice the price. While some Argentine Malbecs appear dark, even to the point of opaque, they are, in fact, often midweight, balanced, and flexible reds. Also Torrontes—a flowery, crisp indigenous white—from La Yunta often tastes better than pricier Viogniers.

Wine Exports

Argentina, one of the largest producers of wine, always had such an enormous domestic market for its product that it didn't worry too much about exports. But that scenario has changed. With competition from beer and soft drinks, the per capita consumption is now around eight gallons a year. While Argentines still consume 95 percent of their domestic wine, exports are on the rise. Foreign and domestic investment has helped the wine industry to improve its product.

Mendoza is Argentina's largest and best wine-producing region. It makes the country's top wines. When Spanish settlers brought vinifera vines to Argentina via Chile and Peru, they discovered that the best place to grow the grapes was at the foot of the Andes. They established the city of Mendoza there in 1561, and it remains the center of Argentina's winemaking industry today.

Malbec has emerged as the country's premier grape. The unheralded grape of Bordeaux has found a home in Argentina and has become the wine industry's signature export.

CANADA

Oh, Canada . . . so often overlooked when it comes to wine. Winemaking in Canada goes back to the 1800s when European settlers tried to grow vinifera grapes in Ontario province. Like their neighbors to the south, the settlers were unsuccessful in their attempts. But the region's native grapes flourished. So, for the next hundred years Canadian winemakers used Vitis labrusca and Vitis riparia and American hybrids and crosses like Niagara, Concord, and Catawba.

By all reports, the wines weren't so great. But when they were made into fortified wines, they became a dependable and lucrative export to England.

Canada Dry?

Around 1900, winemaking started in British Columbia, and *Vitis vinifera* vines were planted again in Canada. But something else was growing as well—a temperance movement that culminated in Canada's Prohibition in

1916. Unlike in the United States, wine wasn't banned and wineries stayed in business. Once Prohibition ended in 1927, the provinces took over control of production, distribution, and sale of alcoholic beverages.

Small wineries had proliferated during Prohibition, reaching sixty-one when Prohibition came to an end. Post-Prohibition, there was a period of consolidation. The bigger companies bought up the small ones so that, by 1974, there were only six wineries in the whole country.

Starting Over

In 1974, the first winery license since Prohibition was awarded to partners Donald Ziraldo and Karl Kaiser who named their boutique winery Inniskillin. Their vision was to produce only the finest wines from traditional vinifera grapes. They were a model for other winemakers and brought Canada into a new era of winemaking.

At the 1991 VinExpo in Bordeaux, Inniskillin won the prestigious Prix d'Honneur for its 1989 Icewine. It was the first of many awards to come for Canadian producers.

$OMMELIER CENTS

fruitful labor

The Canada/USA Free Trade Agreement of 1988 was a catalyst to the Canadian wine industry. The industry was going to have to compete in the world market without government protection. It rose to the challenge to produce premium wines for reasonable prices. The growers of Ontario and British Columbia undertook a major program to replace native grape varieties with vinifera vines throughout their regions.

Hot Ice, Baby

Canada can get cold . . . and stay cold. So much the better to produce ice wines, for which the country has become famous. In fact, Canada is the world's largest producer. Unlike in Germany (where ice wine originated) and Austria, Canadian winters are consistently cold from year to year—guaranteeing that ice wines will be made every year.

Canada makes its best-known whites from Chardonnay, Riesling, and Gewürztraminer as well as Pinot Gris, and Pinot Blanc. Its reds are from Merlot, Pinot Noir, Cabernet Sauvignon, Cabernet Franc, and Gamay.

Through the Grapevine

measuring up

Canada has an appellation system, Vintners Quality Alliance (VQA), similar to France's AOC system. It ensures minimum quality standards through tasting panel testing and by regulating winemaking techniques and grape ripeness. The VQA recognizes three Designated Viticultural Areas in Ontario (Niagara Peninsula, Pelee Island, Lake Erie North Shore) and four in British Columbia (Okanagan Valley, Similkameen Valley, Fraser Valley, Vancouver Island).

NEW FRONTIERS

There's hardly a significant area in the world that doesn't grow grapes for wine. To categorize some of these areas as "new" seems absurd because their winemaking histories go back centuries. China is a good example. Proof exists that its winemaking predates Europe's, but, in terms of modern production, it must be considered New World.

China has about 100 wineries—although wines from vinifera varieties are still a fraction of their production.

Winemaking occurs in other seemingly unlikely places. Turkey is one. In spite of a largely Muslim population that consumes very little wine, Turkey has a strong winemaking industry. It has fifty wineries with total production not much less than Canada. And it surpasses in volume other, more expected, Middle Eastern winemaking countries like Israel and Lebanon. Tunisia, Japan, and Morocco are other examples. Their wines don't make much of a *blip* on the radar screen yet. But who knows what the future holds?

$OMMELIER CENTS

vanishing breeds?

If you're lying awake at night worrying that bargain wines will eventually be nonexistent, rest assured: the barrels will roll on. Why, you ask? The amount of grapes planted keeps increasing, and new—initially less expensive—regions are always being discovered and cultivated. Also, vineyards change hands, and unknown wineries and winemakers are constantly emerging—requiring time to establish a reputation that warrants higher prices.

chapter 5

WINE IN THE UNITED $TATES

. . . .

Virtually since hardy Europeans bounded ashore, America has cultivated vineyards. Even though its modern-day citizens only drink three gallons per person a year—compared to fifteen gallons per person in Italy and France—every one of the fifty states has commercial wineries. Once restricted to regions near bodies of water, today—throughout the USA—in mountains, valleys, and plains, the number of vineyards being cultivated keeps growing and growing.

. . . .

CALIFORNIA

California is, hands down, THE wine state of the United States. It accounts for more than 90 percent of all the wines made in the country and 75 percent of all the wines consumed within its borders! The climate has a lot to do with California's pre-eminence. Not only is it ideal for growing grapes—it also has predictability because there's little variation from year to year. Getting enough sun every year to ripen the grapes is never a problem in California. The challenge is to find cool enough areas so the grapes don't ripen too early without full flavor development.

Wineries have popped up all over the state from the far reaches of the north to the Mexican border in the south. But the regions most conducive to producing wines include:

- **North Coast**—includes Napa, Sonoma, Mendocino, and Lake County
- **Central Coast**—the largest wine area of California (It stretches from San Francisco to Los Angeles. It includes Monterey, Santa Cruz, and Livermore in the northern part and San Luis Obispo and Santa Barbara in the south.)
- **Sierra Foothills**—on the western edge of the Sierra Nevada
- **Central Valley**—includes the vast San Joaquin Valley

"Wine Country"

The Napa Valley and neighboring Sonoma have almost become synonymous with the term *wine country*. Both are famous for their expensive wines, rich history,

78

and breathtaking landscapes, and both are spectacular resources for fine wine and all of its accoutrements.

Napa Valley

Inside the thirty-mile stretch of the Napa Valley, you can eat at elegant gourmet restaurants, get a bite at casual bistros (with a bottle of valley wine, naturally), or just experience the serenity of the valley floor as hot air balloons pass overhead. It's like a fantastic amusement park for adults (with adult prices). And some of the wineries will give you a heck of a ride for your money. The Robert Mondavi Winery alone has ten different tours available. Critics say Napa is too pricey, too crowded, and too ostentatious. But no place else can compare.

Napa has fifteen distinct American Viticultural Areas (AVAs)—with diverse microclimates. It's got cool breezes in the south where it meets the bay, and warms up as you move north. It's got ridgetop vineyards on Mount Veeder with different climate, soil, and exposure than the valley floor vineyards. And it's got well over 200 wineries to take advantage of all the valley's conditions. Some of the Napa AVAs that you'll probably recognize from wine labels are:

- Rutherford
- Howell Mountain
- Atlas Peak
- Mount Veeder
- Oakville
- Spring Mountain
- Stags' Leap District

Cabernet is king in Napa. And while many different varieties are grown, the most produced varietals are Chardonnay, Sauvignon Blanc, Merlot, and Zinfandel.

Sonoma

And then there's Sonoma, California's oldest and second most famous "wine country." It's no Napa. And it doesn't want to be! That's not to say there aren't any wine powerhouses there. (Gallo and Korbel and Kendall-Jackson—all household names—have property in Sonoma.) But Sonoma has a more relaxed personality and more of the character of "Old California."

Sonoma is Napa's western neighbor. Because of its proximity to the Pacific coast, it has a very different climate than Napa. The fog rolls in . . . the fog rolls out. The days are warm, and the nights are cool. Sonoma has lots of AVAs and sub-AVAs. A few of the most notable include:

- **Alexander Valley**—famous for its Cabernets and Chardonnays
- **Russian River Valley**—produces Pinot Noir (thanks to its cooler climate); also known for Chardonnay and sparkling wine
- **Dry Creek Valley**—known for Zinfandel
- **Sonoma Valley and Sonoma Mountain**—produce Cabernet, Pinot Noir, and Chardonnay

$OMMELIER CENTS

raise your label consciousness

Eric Schiffer, President of 99 Cents Only stores, snapped up $15 bottle wines at closeout prices and quickly turned around and sold them for a buck a piece. According to Schiffer, they sold best in a 99 Cents Only store next door to the *very* label-conscious Beverly Hills, where he reported that their closeout wines attracted "the fanciest of our customers."

The wine area of Carneros is a particularly interesting AVA. It's located partly in Sonoma and partly in Napa next to San Pablo Bay, the northern area of San Francisco Bay. It has a cool climate, making it an ideal area for growing Chardonnay and Pinot Noir. The grapes are used in the production of sparkling wines—although dry still wines are produced as well. Because of its climate, Carneros attracted a number of sparkling wine producers from France and Spain who have established wineries there.

Mendocino and Lake County

Dating back to the 1960s, many hippies were drawn to Northern California, where free expression was accepted—and even encouraged. Since then, Northern California has had a reputation for residents who liked to "do their own thing." Mendocino and Lake County are California's northernmost wine-producing areas, and the winemakers there seem to honor their region's hippie heritage by remaining open-minded and experimental about what grapes to grow. They've planted varieties that aren't traditionally associated with California. They're creating wines from Italian varieties like Fiano, Montepulciano, and Arneis and German and French varieties like Riesling, Gewürztraminer, and Pinot Blanc.

Of course, those varieties are in addition to the more traditional, cooler climate grapes of Pinot Noir and Chardonnay. Mendocino is credited with being in the forefront of sustainable agriculture and organic farming.

Sierra Foothills and Livermore Valley

The Sierra Foothills are Gold Rush country. It's mountainous with a cool climate. The most cultivated grapes are Syrah, Zinfandel, and Petite Sirah. But you'll also find Barbera, Sangiovese, and Mourvèdre.

About an hour outside of San Francisco to the south-east lies the Livermore Valley—a historic wine-producing area with a warm and windy climate. It's situated between the cool, marine air of the San Francisco Bay and the hot, dry air of the Central Valley. The French immigrants first planted Sauvignon Blanc and Sémillon there in the 1870s and 1880s. They remain and thrive. Other varieties include Chardonnay, Cabernet Sauvignon, Petite Sirah, and Zinfandel.

The Coastal Regions

The areas within the Central Coast AVA are numerous and disparate. Each one has its own distinctive qualities. Of course, the one with the most current celebrity is the Santa Ynez Valley, north of the town of Santa Barbara.

When a movie made about your region earns an Academy Award nomination—like *Sideways* did in 2005—you can't help but become famous. The premise is two friends set off on a winetasting road trip and discover the pleasures—wine and otherwise—of the Santa Ynez Valley. There are a lot of wine pleasures to experience, from Pinot Noir and Chardonnay to Riesling and Sauvignon Blanc to the Vin Gris from Sanford Winery that the characters spent so much time analyzing.

Central Valley

No fine wine producer brags that its grapes come from the Central Valley. This huge expanse of inland vineyards produces the majority of California's bulk wine—accounting for three-quarters of the state's wine production. (It also grows table grapes and raisins.) But new facilities and technology have improved the wine's quality.

Contemporary California Trendsetters

In the 1980s, some progressive winemakers got tired of producing only Chardonnay and Cabernet Sauvignon.

They wanted to express more of their creativity. In the vein of "everything old becomes new again," they looked to the Old World for inspiration. One group, dubbed the "Rhone Rangers," took their inspiration from southern France and concentrated on making wines from traditional Rhone varieties like Syrah and Viognier.

The idea caught on, and more plantings of those grapes was the result.

Meanwhile, another group of Francophile winemakers wanted to express their creativity in blending—not making one-dimensional varietals. They looked to Bordeaux and its "noble" grapes. The result of their collaboration was Meritage wines and the Meritage Association.

Meritage wines have to blend at least two of the Bordeaux varieties, and no single variety can make up more than 90 percent of the blend. Some excellent Meritage wines, both red and white, are now produced across the United States.

What's Next?

Because winemaking practices and the popular enjoyment of wine are cyclical, you can probably look to history for the answer. One trend seems to be the shift away from heavily oaked California wines. For twenty-five years, California winemakers were fascinated with oak and used a lot of it. On another continent, the wine-producing regions of France—like the Loire Valley and Rhone—have always relied on the true taste of the fermented grape and have met with popular approval. Today, California winemakers are making the move to create softer, more fruit-driven wine—with little or no oak.

NEW YORK

New York is the second largest wine-producing state in the United States, but it often gets overlooked in the mind of the public—maybe because of the overwhelming presence of California. Until 1960, New York wines came from native American varieties like Concord, Catawba, Niagara, and Delaware and hybrid grapes such as Seyval Blanc and Baco Noir. The hybrids, in particular, are still produced, but the more popular vinifera wines have usurped their position.

The Finger Lakes

For years it was accepted that New York winters were too cold for vinifera vines to survive. Enter a Russian immigrant, Dr. Konstantin Frank. Dr. Frank had organized a collective farm and taught viticulture in his native Ukraine. When he came to the United States in 1951, he took a job at the New York State Agricultural Experiment Station, where he observed the lack of vinifera vines in the Finger Lakes area. When he asked why, he was given the expected answer. But Frank had already grown vinifera grapes successfully in the Ukraine where winters were much colder. So he set out to prove his point and, in 1953, succeeded in growing Riesling in Hammondsport, New York.

Today, the Finger Lakes region is an officially recognized AVA—whose Rieslings compare favorably with their European counterparts. The area encompasses 4,000 square miles and has 15,000 acres of vines. The area has more than seventy wineries of all sizes—including Constellation Brands (formerly Canandaigua), one of the world's largest wine suppliers. Finger Lakes producers do particularly well with Riesling, Chardonnay, Pinot Noir, sparkling wines, and ice wines.

Hudson River Valley

North of New York City along the majestic Hudson River is the historic Hudson Valley. It was a pioneering region for French-American hybrids such as Seyval Blanc and Baco Noir. These days it also grows Chardonnay and Cabernet Franc. The area has more than twenty wineries including the oldest continuously running winery in the country. Brotherhood Winery produced the first commercial vintage in 1839. It was able to keep its doors open through Prohibition by making sacramental wine.

Long Island

The Finger Lakes and Hudson Valley may have a rich past, but New York's Long Island has a bright future. In 1973, when Alex and Louisa Hargrave were looking for a suitable place to plant some grapevines, somebody suggested checking out Long Island. The maritime microclimate, it was said, was very similar to Bordeaux.

After researching and soil testing—but mostly because of intuition—the Hargraves put down roots on seventeen acres of the island's North Fork. Two years later they bottled their first wines and released them in 1977. Today, thirty-eight wineries are producing wines from grapes on 3,000 acres of land—including quality Merlot, Cabernet, Cabernet Franc, Chardonnay, and more.

OREGON

Although wines were made in Oregon in the nineteenth century, Prohibition effectively wiped out the entire wine industry. Oregon's wine pioneers arrived in the 1960s. At the time no vinifera vines were planted. They brought enthusiasm, new ideas, and, in some cases, degrees from UC Davis.

Oregon's climate is marked by cool growing seasons . . . and plenty of rain. It presents challenges—but nothing Oregon's new winemakers didn't think they could overcome. They just had to be discerning about where and how they planted their vineyards. Unlike in California where sprawling vineyard tracts were the norm, Oregon vineyards were planted in small pockets to take advantage of the best weather conditions.

Pinot Noir Takes Root

Oregon's location, along the 45th parallel, in addition to its maritime weather, make the growing climate very similar to that of Burgundy, France. One of Oregon's pioneers, David Lett of Eyrie Vineyard, was convinced that the traditional grapes of Burgundy could grow well in Oregon—and certainly grow better than they did in California. He planted the first Pinot Noir vines in 1965. A decade or so later, his Pinot Noir wines would put Oregon on the map of the wine world.

Oregon's Other Pinot

Pinot Noir's companion grape in Burgundy is Chardonnay, and it's no stranger to Oregon. But the real success story in the white wine category in Oregon in Pinot Gris. Again, thanks to David Lett, Pinot Gris was introduced to the region in 1965 and has since been adopted by winemakers across the state.

The style of Oregon's Pinot Gris has been compared to that made in Alsace, but subtle variations exist. And it's entirely different than the Pinot Grigio wines made from the same grape. In general, Oregon's Pinot Gris is medium-bodied, yellow to copper pink in color, crisp, with full fruit flavors. The wines from Alsace are medium- to full-bodied, slightly floral, and less fruity. Pinot Grigio—from almost everywhere—is light-bodied, light in color, and neutral in flavor.

Growing Regions

Oregon has nine officially recognized AVAs—three of them shared with neighboring Washington State—and six more in the works. Among them are the following:

- **Willamette Valley**—The largest and most important region. This fertile river valley is located directly south of Portland in the northwest end of the state. It produces primarily Pinot Noir, Pinot Gris, Chardonnay, and Riesling.

- **Umpqua Valley**—The site of Oregon's first winery, Hillcrest Vineyard. South of the Willamette Valley, it has a warm climate and produces Chardonnay, Pinot Noir, Cabernet Sauvignon, Riesling, and Sauvignon Blanc.
- **Rogeue Valley**—This area is further south, with a dry, warm climate. Varietals include Pinot Gris, Riesling, Chardonnay, and Gewürztraminer.
- **Applegate Valley**—This region falls within the Rogue Valley. It produces Cabernet Franc, Sémillon, Cabernet Sauvignon, and Merlot.

WASHINGTON

Like Oregon, Washington was late getting into the wine business. Washington's two largest wineries—Columbia Winery and Château Ste. Michelle—planted the first commercial-scale vineyards in the 1960s. But even so, it wasn't until the '80s that most of the growth started. Today Washington has over 320 wineries.

Also like Oregon, the state is divided by the north-south Cascade Mountains. West of the mountain range the climate is cool with plenty of rain and vegetation. To the east of the mountains the land is desertlike: hot, dry summers and cold winters. Ninety-eight percent of the state's grapes grow east of the mountains.

Because of its northerly location, Washington gets lots of summer sun—two more hours of summer sunlight each day than in California regions. It's great for ripening the grapes. The cool autumn temperatures help the grapes maintain desirable acid levels as they reach maturity. In terms of volume, Washington produces more wine grapes than any state except California.

Wine Regions

Five of Washington's six official wine regions are in the arid east, where irrigation made commercial vine growing possible. They are:

- **Yakima Valley**—Washington's very first AVA, it now has more than forty wineries. The most widely planted grapes are Chardonnay, followed by Merlot and Cabernet and significant acreage of Riesling and Syrah.
- **Columbia Valley**—The largest region in Washington, it represents a full third of Washington's landmass. Production of Merlot is followed by Cabernet, Chardonnay, Riesling, and Syrah.
- **Walla Walla Valley**—This AVA is shared with Oregon. It has more than fifty-five wineries and produces Cabernet Sauvignon, Merlot, Chardonnay, Syrah, Gewürztraminer, Cabernet Franc, and Sangiovese.
- **Red Mountain**—Located at the east end of the Yakima Valley, it's known for its red varietals: Cabernet, Merlot, Cabernet Franc, Syrah, and Sangiovese.
- **Columbia Gorge**—The newest AVA, part of the appellation is shared with Oregon. It produces Chardonnay, Gewürztraminer, Riesling, and Pinot Gris.

The sixth AVA is Puget Sound near Seattle. It has eighty vineyard acres of vinifera grapes and about thirty-five wineries. Many of the larger wineries are located in this area but obtain almost all their grapes from the Columbia and Yakima Valleys.

ELSEWHERE IN THE USA

California, New York, and the Northwest may be the big wine players in the United States, but every state has its own unique wine story to tell. Take Missouri, for example. In the 1860s, Missouri made more wine than California and New York combined! The influx of German immigrants to Hermann, an hour and a half west of St. Louis, on the banks of the Missouri River, made the area known as the Rhineland of Missouri. But the wines produced weren't made from German grapes. No Riesling in sight. Ageworthy reds are made from Norton and Cynthiana, and whites are made with Vignoles, Seyval Blanc, and Vidal Blanc.

Deep in the Heart of Texas

The Lone Star State comes in at number five in wine production—right after California, New York, Washington, and Oregon. Texas developed a close association with France during the 1880s phylloxera epidemic. A French scientist, Pierre Viala, from Cognac was sent to Texas to try to find a cure for the vineyard plague. He traveled to Denison, Texas, because the soil composition there was similar to that in Cognac and should have grape species capable of growing in both places. Viala was introduced to Thomas Volney Munson, a Texas scientist who knew Texas rootstocks were resistant to phylloxera. At Munson's suggestion Viala shipped the Texas rootstocks back to France where they were grafted to French vines. For his contribution to France, Munson was given the highest honor awarded to a foreign civilian, the Chevalier du Merite Agricole.

New Mexico Stands Proud

While every U.S. state can proudly boast of its wines—and rightfully so—a few states can claim top wine titles. New Mexico, a state not known for wine, can brag of its sparklings, particularly Gruet. The Gruet family produces six different sparkling wines. Their vineyards are located at 4,300 feet—some of the highest in the United States—which helps to produce grapes good for sparkling wines.

chapter 6

FEELING YOUR GRAPES

. . . .

If you're like millions of people, you know what kind of wine you like when you taste it, but you just don't have a sharp memory for names, nor confidence in your ability to pronounce it. Determining why you enjoy one wine over another and expressing yourself articulately can be easily learned. It's simply a matter of tasting wines, taking notes, practicing pronunciations, and learning a few insider words or phrases that will effectively communicate your true savoir-faire to the wine salesperson.

. . . .

MR. CHEAP

ACQUIRING WINE SAVOIR-FAIRE

Let's hone in on some basics, shall we? First of all, taste is subjective—whether you're talking about art, fashion, music, or wine. Of course, with wine, there's also a physiological dimension to how we taste. No two people experience taste in exactly the same way. And because of our upbringing and cultural influences, we've learned to appreciate certain flavors.

Our own taste can change from day to day and from place to place. That incredible bottle of Chianti you shared over a romantic dinner didn't measure up when you drank it alone in front of the TV, did it? Your taste is affected by your mood, by your health, and by your environment. Try to enjoy a floral Viognier when you have a cold or when you're in a smoke-filled room. It will be quite a challenge.

What you taste is really a composite of four sensations: sight, smell, taste, and touch.

Sight

A wine's appearance influences your judgment. The color: Is it what you expected . . . or is it somehow "off"? The clarity: Is there any cloudiness that would indicate the wine is unfined? Or are there any tartrate crystals that might need decanting? In blind wine tastings, participants are sometimes given black, opaque glasses so they're not prejudiced by what the wine looks like—even whether it's red or white.

Smell

Our sense of smell is our most acute—and a thousand times more sensitive than our sense of taste. You sense aromas either directly by inhaling through your nose or, indirectly, through the interior nasal passage at the back of your mouth. What we experience when we "taste" wine is actually 75 percent smell and only 25 percent taste. Wine is made up of over 200 different chemical compounds. Many of them are similar—or identical—to those in fruits, vegetables, flowers, herbs, and spices. So it's not surprising to hear someone say, "I smell peaches" over a glass of Riesling.

Taste

In contrast to the multitude of aromas the nose can identify, the tongue recognizes only four basic tastes: sweetness, saltiness, acidity, and bitterness. Saltiness doesn't come into play when tasting wine, but the others are critical. The tip of the tongue registers sweetness first. Acidity, in the form of a sour taste, registers along the sides of the tongue. And bitterness is recognized at the back of the tongue near the throat.

Sweetness and acidity are the yin and yang of the wine tasting world. They balance each other. Think of lemonade. Lemon juice on its own is a mouth-puckering experience. The more sugar you add to the juice, the less you notice the acidity.

Touch

Wines have texture that you can feel in your mouth.
A wine can be thin—like water. Or it can be full—like
cream. That's what a wine's "body" is all about. "Full-
bodied" and "light-bodied" aren't value judgments . . .
they're descriptions.

Your mouth distinguishes other sensations as well.
Tannins, the elements responsible for a wine's ability to
age, have an astringent, mouth drying effect very much
like the impression you get when you drink over-steeped
tea. And the alcohol in the wine will give you a hot feeling at your throat and on the roof of your mouth.

PRO-LIFTING:
TASTING WINE LIKE A PRO

There's nothing wrong with simply picking up your glass
of wine and taking a swig. But for the full experience,
you might want to copy what professional wine tasters
do. They employ certain techniques that can magnify
the sensations—and the enjoyment—of the wine.

Swirling

You know how to swirl, don't you . . . just pick
up your glass and whirl it around. The wine will rotate
and spin and release its aromas into the air. (And you

thought swirling was just some snobbish pretension!) Before the aromas escape and are lost, stick your nose right into the glass. Inhale deeply. Yes, it's much more than a sniff. Breathe it in.

And now, do it again. You can't possibly take in all the aroma nuances at once. Close your eyes. What scents are you detecting? You may smell something new each time.

And that's the fun.

Swishing and Slurping

Aromas, as seductive as they are, are still prelude. It's time to taste. Wine pros savor the moment. No quick swallow here. Swish the wine around in your mouth. Touch every surface of your tongue with wine. Hit every taste receptor.

You're not done yet. Purse your lips and draw in some air across the wine on your tongue. We know—it sounds gross. It's called slurping because, well, that's how it sounds. It aerates and oxidizes the wine so that you can smell/taste it through your rear nasal passage.

You're probably ready to swallow the wine right about now. Not so fast. Many professionals take this opportunity to spit. Yes, you heard right . . . spit. While most of us are loath to waste good wine that way, professional tasters have to keep their wits about them for the next wine (and there could be hundreds). So into the dump bucket goes a mouthful of wine. Amateurs, however, need not feel obligated to follow this step.

___

Through the Grapevine

my glass is only 1/3 full

Don't even think about swirling with a full glass of wine! The glass should be no more than one-third full. There's got to be enough room between the level of the liquid and the top of the glass for the vapors to accumulate. Besides, any more than a third full and you'll have a hefty dry-cleaning bill.

TALKING THE TALK

When wine lovers get excited about a new wine find, they want to share the experience. The only trouble is, words are so inadequate. But let's face it: Words are the best tools we have—short of handing out wine samples to everyone—to communicate our enthusiasm. Talking about wine has become intimidating, probably because wine snobs use words in such a way that it makes them mysterious and pretentious. Talk about wine any way you want in order to convey your meaning. If you want to compare a full-bodied wine to a Rubens painting, go for it. But there are some words used in wine descriptions that are good to know. Even if you never use them, you'll understand what's being said when other people use them. Some of the most frequently used words:

- **Dry**—It's the opposite of sweet. When all the sugar in the grape juice has been converted to alcohol and carbon dioxide, the wine is said to be bone-dry. Of course, there's lots of room in the continuum between sweet and dry. If enough residual sugar remains to give the wine a slight sweetness, it's called off-dry.

- **Balance**—None of the wine's components is out-of-whack. The acid, alcohol, fruit, and tannins all work together so that one doesn't stand apart from the rest.
- **Finish**—A wine's aftertaste, or the flavor or aroma that lingers after you've swallowed the wine, is referred to as its *finish*. If it has one, it's considered a good thing—and the longer the better. A "long finish" is a real compliment.
- **Complex**—Layers and nuances of flavor make a wine complex. A complex wine will continue to reveal itself as you sip it. This multidimensional quality is often achieved with aging. A complex wine is also said to have depth.
- **Fruity**—Fruit flavors—besides grapes—perceived in a wine make it "fruity." Blackberries, strawberries, and currants are just a few of the fruity flavors you can detect in wines. You notice them as the taste of the wine evolves. If they hit you—BANG!—as soon as you take the first sip, the term to use is *fruit-forward*.
- **Crisp**—A wine with good acidity and taste and no excessive sweetness is crisp. Think of an apple. The wine is relatively high in acidity, but the acidity doesn't overwhelm the other components.

In general some of the flavors you'll be able to discern from white wines are melon, apple, pineapple, pear, citrus, vanilla, caramel, flowers, herbs, grass, minerals, olives, and mushrooms. Some flavors from red wines are berries, peaches, currants, plums, cherries, oranges, flowers, earth, wood, smoke, chocolate, tobacco, leather, and coffee.

RECOGNIZING "FLAWS"

When you taste a wine you know if you like it. You can't always explain why. Maybe you don't even care about identifying the specific flavor characteristics that make the wine so tasty. You just want to sip and enjoy. But how about when you don't like the wine? You smell or taste it and . . . yuck! Is it just you? Are you particularly sensitive to a certain aroma?

Wines can be defective if they're not carefully made or if they're improperly handled or stored. Recognizing flaws isn't always black-and-white. There's no clear dividing line between good and bad wine. It's a matter of degree. Certain characteristics that make a wine flawed can actually, in small amounts, be considered by some people to be a plus. It's similar to adding garlic to food: A little bit enhances the dish, but too much ruins it. Recognizing flaws takes knowing what to look for. When you know the telltale signs, you'll know when it's bad.

Corks

Your wine smells of damp cardboard or musty basement. Whether the odor is pronounced or just slightly dank, it came from a cork tainted with a chemical compound called TCA. When the wine is damaged in this way, it's said to be corked. By industry estimates, 2 to 7 percent of all wines are corked. Cork processing improvements have been made to eliminate TCA production, but wineries are looking elsewhere—like to screw tops—for permanent remedies. When a wine is corked, it's bad.

Oxygen

The wine tastes dull, cooked, or a little Sherry-like. A white wine has an off color—brownish or dark yellow. These are all indications that the wine has been exposed to oxygen sometime during its life.

It could have happened while the wine was being made or when it was being stored. If wines are stored upright for long periods instead of on their sides, the cork can dry out and let air into the bottle. Wines with low acidity will smell cooked. Wines with high acidity will smell burned.

Perhaps your wine smells like vinegar or nail polish remover. This is an extreme case having to do with oxygen in the presence of a vinegar-producing bacterium called *acetobacter*. Acetobacter is everywhere—on grape skins, winery walls, and barrels. By itself, it has no aroma or flavor. But when it meets oxygen in winemaking, it produces both acetic acid (the vinegar aroma) and ethyl acetate (the smell of nail polish remover). When this happens (it's called volatile acidity), the wine is bad.

Through the Grapevine

the anti-vinegar

Many people assume that when a wine gets too old, it turns to vinegar. More likely, it will become dull and take on a nutty taste. Thanks to Louis Pasteur's groundbreaking work on fermentation, winemakers learned to keep wines out of contact with air and bacteria during the production process. As a result, a wine turning to vinegar has become a rarity.

Yeast

Your wine smells like a barnyard. It may be the result of a yeast called brettanomyces—brett, for short.

Brett grows on grapes and in wineries and is next to impossible to get rid of. Winemakers use special filters to help reduce its growth. Some wine drinkers enjoy a low level of brett, maintaining that it adds complexity to the wine's aroma. But you know what they say about too much of a good thing. The wine is bad.

Through the Grapevine

wow, look at those legs!
Ever wonder what it means when an expert talks about a wine's legs? When you swirl a glass of wine, little streams of wine fall back down the sides of the glass. These are the legs. Some people draw conclusions from them about the wine's quality. But, bottom line: The "better" the legs, the higher the alcohol content.

Sulfur Dioxide

Your wine smells like water from a sulfur spring. Winemakers add sulfur dioxide to preserve the wine. But too much and the odor is evident. You'll find this most often in cheap white wines. The wine is bad.

Heat

The wine is brown, and it smells like it's been cooked. In Madeira, this is a plus and part of the wine's essential character. In other wines, it's a flaw. It happens mostly to white and Rosé wines. The term to describe this condition is maderized. The wine has likely experienced severe fluctuations of temperature in a short period of time or been stored in heat. Sometimes the cork will be pushed up a little. The wine is bad.

Style Preferences

What you like in a wine, the next person might hate. Too much yeast? Too much oak? Too much acid? Personal preferences don't reflect a failure in the winemaking process. The fact that you don't like a wine doesn't mean it's flawed. It's not bad. Chalk it up to a bad choice.

DO CRITICS KNOW BEST?

Wine ratings are like movie reviews. Just because a wine critic has anointed a bottle of California Cabernet with a perfect score of 100 doesn't mean that it will win an Academy Award at your house over dinner.

$OMMELIER CENTS

keep an ear to the ground

Even when they've released a spectacular vintage that garnered high ratings in the press, small producers often don't have the overhead or promotional budget that spikes their original prices. If they produced 40,000+ cases, it may be worth pursuing. If the inventory is under 1,000 cases, it's a lost cause, but keep your eyes and ears open for the next one.

In your lifetime you've probably seen hundreds—if not thousands—of movies. You've developed a set of likes and dislikes. You like love stories, and you hate kickboxing movies. Based on your personal preferences, you decide what new movies you'll spend your hard-earned cash to see. So even if Roger Ebert gives a thumbs-up to the latest Jackie Chan flick, there's no way you're going to see it. You're confident about your movie choices because you have a basis of experience.

For many people wine is a completely different story. They haven't had the experience of tasting thousands of wines in order to develop a catalog of personal taste preferences. So they look to experts for guidance.

The Experts

Wine reviews come in all shapes and sizes, as do the delivery methods. There are individual reviewers, panel reports, and wine competitions. You can read them in newspapers, magazines, on "shelf talkers" and even on the back labels of bottles. Some are more helpful and reliable than others.

Without question, the wine world's most influential critic is Robert Parker. He first published his monthly newsletter, the *Wine Advocate,* in 1978 and introduced the 100-point scale for rating wines. The rating scale has been widely imitated ever since.

Parker's influence is measurable. When he gives a wine a high score, the price goes up and availability goes down. Some producers in Bordeaux wait for Parker's scores before they set the release price of their wines. And his ratings have been instrumental in creating Napa's famous cult wines. The term *Parkerization* was coined to refer to wines that are made with the intention of earning Parker points by creating the kinds of wines he likes—rich, thick, ripe, and oaky. This underscores the importance of knowing a reviewer's taste preferences before following his advice. Not all reviewers are created equal. But, collectively, they've raised the public's consciousness about wine and its enjoyment.

Reviewers: How to Spot a Good One

Knowledge is power, and anyone who hopes to score good wine at exceptional prices needs a sophisticated ally. Magazine, newspaper, and Internet reviewers are readily available to serve as powerful allies, as are trusted friends, but how do you know if their informed opinions are the "right fit" for you?

- **Knowledge.** They have superior knowledge or instincts when it comes to everything wine.
- **Consistency.** They consistently provide top-drawer reviews—honest, fair, descriptive, and right on target.
- **Impartiality.** They don't favor advertisers, and consistently seek out great wines—remaining indifferent to whether they have the bucks to advertise or not.
- **Diversity.** They cover a wide range of varietals, producers, and prices.
- **Objectivity.** They aren't plying their favorites, or displaying blatant biases.
- **Adventuresome.** They go outside their comfort range to find surprises for you.
- **Simpatico.** Their taste level is in accordance with yours.

Rating Systems

Robert Parker's ratings are based on single-blind, peer-group tastings, which means that the same type wines are tasted at the same time without tasters' knowledge of who the wine producers are.

Each wine automatically get 50 points—maybe just for the effort that went into making it. Color and appearance can earn up to 5 points. Aroma can get 15 points. Flavor and finish merit up to 20 points. And the overall quality can earn up to 10.

While other wine authorities such as *Wine Spectator* magazine also use the 100-point scale in their tastings, it's not the only one in use. *Decanter* magazine, an esteemed wine periodical in England, employs a 1-to-5 star rating. English wine writer Clive Coates uses a 20-point system. And Dorothy Gaiter and John Brecher, the much-admired *Wall Street Journal* columnists, use simply, "Good/Very Good/Delicious/Delicious!" Some reviewers don't use a rating system at all, preferring narrative descriptions based on their tasting notes.

$OMMELIER CENTS

rate this!

Another rating system—Quality/Price Ratio (QPR)—is becoming popular. It measures the correlation between what a wine sells for and its relative quality. A score of 100 percent means the price matches the quality. A score under 100 percent means you're getting a good deal for your money. A score over 100 percent means you're paying too much.

Rating the Vintages

Not only wines get rated. Vintages get rated too. The years that the grapes are harvested get scores in the form of vintage charts. Wine-growing regions have different weather conditions every year—some with dramatic fluctuations—that affect wine quality. The charts direct you to the best years for each region or subregion.

Vintage charts range from basic to detailed, from one person's evaluation to a collective judgment, and from noted experts to your local retailer. Chart authors give each region a numerical score (as is done with individual wines) and map them on a grid to indicate the potential of that area's wine for that year. More comprehensive charts will tell you whether to hold the wine for aging or drink it now—or whether it's past its peak.

Even in the best years, a mediocre wine can show up. And in a so-so year, a talented winemaker can produce a very good wine. So instead of focusing entirely on vintage ratings, look at the track record of a winery over a period of years.

It Was a Very Good Year . . .

Wine critics have a grip on reality. They're not going to recommend wines that no one can afford (at least not all the time). Here are some inexpensive and some expensive (for the splurge occasions) wine suggestions from the experts:

- Bonterra North Coast Cabernet Sauvignon 2001 (Robin Garr)—$17
- Rudera Chenin Blanc 2002 (Tom Cannavan—*www.wine-pages.com*)—$22
- Carmen Carmenère-Cabernet Reserve Maipo Valley 2001 (*Decanter magazine*)—$14
- Villa Maria Reserve Marlborough Pinot Noir 2003 (Sue Courtney—*www.wineoftheweek.com*)—$45

- Porcupine Ridge Syrah 2003 (Jancis Robinson)—$13
- William Fevre Chablis 2002 (Jamie Goode—*www.wineanorak.com*)—$25
- Catena Malbec 2002 (*Wine Spectator* magazine)—$23
- Lamborghini Campoleone 1999 (Robert Parker)—$79

Through the Grapevine

listen up!

Check out Grape Radio (*www.graperadio.com*), where "the Grape Bunch" makes learning about wine interactive and fun. From their quizzes to their podcasts, they uplift your spirits while increasing your knowledge. They have an extensive list of wine-related topics listenable in twenty-minute segments, ranging from interviews with winemakers and wine celebrities to discussing their own preferences.

When it comes to enjoying wine—no matter what the vintage year, no matter what the critics say—it's ultimately up to you. Your personal preferences will guide you to make the right selections.

chapter 7

THE 411 ON WHY WINE IS EXPEN$IVE

. . . .

You're standing in front of a shelf of Cabernets wondering whether to buy the $10 bottle or the $50 bottle. Your wallet says go for the cheaper one; your palate seriously ponders whether the more expensive bottle is five times better. A bottle of wine acquires costs at every stage of its life—from the vineyard to the table. Knowing all the costs will guide you toward realistic expectations and, ultimately, a reasonable decision. So, let's discuss all the elements that go into creating a three-tier market price, shall we?

. . . .

TIER ONE: THE WINEMAKERS

Although it may often appear to be so, whether or not one bottle of wine sells for $10 and another for $50 has nothing to do with chance. Winemakers can choose whether they want to make their wines cheaply or expensively. There are lots of variables that go into pricing wine—but it all begins with the grapes.

Location, Location, Location

Growing grapes takes land. Like any real estate, the watchwords for vineyard land are "location, location, location." Some properties are ideal for growing grapes: good soil, proper drainage, good breezes, and the right sun exposure. Of course, not all vineyard land is created equal. Some properties, because of the cachet they acquire, command top dollar. The Napa Valley is a perfect example. In 1960 you could have bought an acre of vineyard land there for $2,000. Today, the average price per acre is $200,000. Not all vineyard land is that exorbitant. Elsewhere in the United States and certainly in areas like South America, you'll find affordable land for growing grapes. The cost of the vineyard land goes into your bottle of wine.

$OMMELIER CENTS

bragging rights

Winemakers who produce high-end wines aren't usually whining about the low yields of their vineyards—in fact, they often brag about it! It's not uncommon to hear about yields of less than a ton of grapes per acre. Contrast this to the grapes headed for the lower-priced wines. The yields can be from six tons per acre up to ten tons per acre. One ton of grapes generally reaps about 740 bottles of wine.

How the grapes are grown affects price. It stands to reason that the more grapes you grow on an acre of land, the more wine you can make. On the other hand, it's generally agreed that lower yields produce better quality grapes and more concentrated flavors in the juice. So producers of high-quality wines seek to lower yields even though it will result in less juice. A winemaker who grows grapes in high-yielding vineyards will harvest the grapes by machine with minimum labor cost. To achieve lower yields, another winemaker will thin the vines—meaning she'll remove whole clusters of grapes—by hand. The cost of the bottle goes up again.

the year of the grape!

When it's a good year for grapes in any appellation, it's a lucky year for wine lovers. Any winery that has a sharp winemaker on staff will likely produce an excellent wine in excess quantities. Even if their product has taken a delightful leap in quality, wineries often opt to keep prices low to guarantee that they'll deplete the excess inventory. Savvy wine buyers will reap the benefits by snapping up cases during such stellar years.

The Price of Grapes

Winemakers who don't grow their own grapes buy them from other growers. The price they pay depends on the grape variety, the location of the vineyard and, of course, supply and demand. In 2003, Cabernet grapes from Napa Valley sold for about $4,000 per ton compared to about $1,200 for Cabernet grapes from Washington and about $300 for grapes from California's Central Valley.

Grape variety makes a difference. A less-in-demand grape will cost less. In the same year the Cabernet grapes from Napa sold for $4,000 a ton, other grape varieties from the same region had lower price tags. Chardonnay grapes went for $2,300, Pinot Noir grapes went for $2,200, and Riesling grapes sold for $1,800. That too is reflected in the price of your chosen bottle.

From Vine to Wine

Pressing, fermenting, finishing, and aging all contribute to price. One winemaker might squeeze as much juice as possible out of the grapes and then ferment it in huge tanks—filtering and bottling after only a few weeks. Another producer might use minimal pressing, using only the free-run juice, and ferment and age the wine in oak barrels.

Oak is a major cost. American oak barrels sell for about $300, while French oak goes for $750. Barrels hold about 280 bottles of wine. So just aging in French oak could add more than $2.50 to what you pay for the wine. Barrels lose their potency with use, and they have to be replaced. Makers of high-end wines replace them every year.

To Age or Not to Age?

Once the wine is produced, the question for the winemaker is whether or not to age the wine—and, if so, for how long? The longer the wine ages, the longer it sits without producing income . . . and the longer it will take for the winemaker to recoup her costs. Since it could be years down the road, ageing wine drives up the price.

Dressing to Sell

When wines are ready for bottling, distinctive packaging is a must. The bottle itself can start at fifty cents and go up to $2 for a thicker, higher-quality version. Corks can cost anywhere from ten cents to $1.

stack them up!
A typical oak barrel holds sixty gallons and is about twice the size of a typical garbage can. It could take 150 barrels to accommodate the volume of a single stainless steel tank. And to hold all those barrels requires an enormous temperature-controlled warehouse, which drives up the price of genuine oak barrel aging.

The wine needs a label. First, someone has to design it. Then, the labels have to be printed—at twenty to thirty cents apiece. And before the wine goes out the door, it goes into a cardboard case, which can cost up to $7.

Why Some Wines Are Overpriced

Expensive wines are not always superior to their lesser-priced brothers and sisters. In fact, the price of wine can escalate for reasons completely separate from taste or quality. Some reasons certain wines cost more:

- **Winery cachet.** The legendary status of the Rothschild family wineries makes many not only expect, but willing to pay, exorbitant prices.
- **Famous owners.** Francis Ford Coppola—need we say more!
- **Celebrated winemakers.** Someone who has gained stature based on his or her ability to consistently create great wine adds bucks to whatever they produce.
- **Regional attraction.** The Bordeaux region in France and the Napa Valley's legendary Cabernet regions garner elevated price points.

- **Availability.** Limited production or distribution can create unheralded demand that skyrockets prices. Ditto for wines that are sold out at the winery but available at retail. Some retailers and restaurants will raise prices to slow sales—to maintain a reserve of highly desirable, yet unavailable, wines that bolster their image and lure buyers through the door.
- **Aging.** The longer wine is aged in oak barrels, the longer it takes for a winery to turn a profit. Also, aging 100 percent in oak barrels, and even where the barrels are made, can boost the price significantly, but it's often well worth the price.
- **Prizes.** Any wine that wins a gold medal in competitions can boost their prices immediately.
- **Keeping up with eBay.** If the value rises, retailers want to discourage buyers from snapping up their product only to turn around and sell it on eBay.
- **Packaging.** If a winery hires a prominent artist to design its labels or fancy packaging, the extra cost is built into the product.
- **Psychological appeal.** If a wine is attractively packaged, promoted, and expensive, we all expect it to taste superior.

The Pricing Game

The winery has measurable production costs that it has to cover if it's going to stay in business. But, in setting a price for the wine, there are other matters to consider. One is the winery's profit. How does the producer allocate that on a per-bottle basis? It will depend on how many bottles it produced. The fewer bottles the winery has to sell, the more it has to charge per bottle. If

MR. CHEAP'S GUIDE TO WINE

the winery has lots to sell, the volume will make up for a smaller per-bottle margin.

Another consideration is the perceived value of the wine. The winery wants to position its wine at a price that's in line with other wines of the same caliber and stature. If the producer prices it too high, consumers will buy other wines instead. If the producer prices it too low, not only will the company lose money, but it will hurt the reputation of the wine as well. The winery's goal is to price it high enough to attract serious wine drinkers, but low enough to make sure it all gets sold.

$OMMELIER CENTS

a wine by any name

Although the original "garage wine" came from novices creating personal wines in their garages, when Le Pin, a small winery in Bordeaux, France, produced an exceptional 1981 vintage—using grapes from a five-acre plot that they fermented in the basement of an old farmhouse—other wineries quickly followed suit. Their small-batch, high-quality wines were called by many names: boutique wines, micro-wine, micro-cuvee, and cult wine, for example. Because you are frequently paying for cachet, these wines can burn your pocketbook, so buy sparingly and save for very special occasions.

The High Cost of Selling

If you were around in the '70s, you'll remember Orson Welles and his "Sell no wine before its time" television commercials. Today, the big, branded wines like Woodbridge, Turning Leaf, and Arbor Mist do significant advertising, but most wineries are small and can't afford the millions required to get results. In 2002, wineries collectively spent $122.4 million on advertising. That's a drop in the bucket compared to other industries.

Wineries have marketing expenses, of course, including tasting rooms, sales staffs, and promotions. The reality of how wines are sold—through distributors in each state—means that most of a winery's marketing efforts are directed toward building relationships with those wholesalers.

The cost of a wine is not the best indicator of quality. Admittedly, many production and aging processes are expensive. But beyond a certain point, there are really no differences in the cost of production. If you shell out more than about $30 for a bottle of wine, you're paying for the prestige.

TIER TWO: THE MIDDLEMEN

After Prohibition ended, state and federal laws went into effect that separated the activities of the producers of wine (and all alcoholic beverages) and the activities of the sellers, namely the retailers. Enter the distributor or wholesaler—the middleman, creating what is known as the three-tier system for conducting business. Tier-one is the wine producers; let's discuss the tier-two and tier-three players.

$OMMELIER CENTS

a taxing situation

States impose taxes on wine, and they go into the price you pay. The average state excise tax is sixty-four cents a gallon—the highest being Alaska at $2.50 a gallon and the lowest being Louisiana at eleven cents a gallon. And don't forget state and local sales taxes. With state budget deficits, many states are considering increasing taxes and fees on alcohol to supplement their income.

Enter the Wholesaler

Say a California winery (tier one) wants to sell its wine in Tennessee. It shops around for a wholesaler (tier two), chooses the one that provides the best deal, and starts shipping wine. The wholesaler sells the wine to retailers (tier three) and restaurants and pays the state the appropriate excise taxes. The retailer then sells the wine to the consumer.

In the process, the wholesaler:

- Ships the wine to its warehouse from the winery
- Stores the wine in its warehouse
- Sells the wine to stores and restaurants
- Delivers the wine to purchasers

A wholesale operation requires people, buildings, and equipment. While markups will vary, a wholesaler will add about 30 percent to 40 percent to the cost of your wine.

The Tax Man Cometh

Every state has a different way of implementing the three-tier system. Some states have state-controlled liquor boards that act as wholesalers. Some states, like Pennsylvania, also assume the retailer role with their state-run stores. State laws may mandate price posting and specify markups, or prohibit quantity discounts and deliveries to retailers' distribution centers.

Some state laws regulate in-state and out-of-state wineries differently. Many states allow in-state wineries to sell directly to consumers but won't allow out-of-state wineries to do the same. Some states allow their own wineries to sell directly to retailers but, again, prohibit out-of-state wineries from taking part in the same activity.

These practices have been the basis in the last several years of litigation to open up free trade for wine between the states. Twenty-four states prohibit direct shipment of wine to consumers. A coalition of smaller, family-owned wineries has argued that the system prevents them from engaging in interstate commerce.

The Internet Revolution

Wineries have always objected to the direct shipping prohibition, but until the advent of the Internet, it was not much more than an irritant to wine drinkers. The power of the Internet to get online merchandise delivered to homes overnight has revolutionized the way people think about free trade and getting the best products at the best prices. These days, with thousands of Web sites selling wines that aren't available anywhere else, interstate shipping of wine has become a national obsession.

There are about 25,000 different wines that are available for sale to consumers in the United States. But only about 500 of them have access to the crowded distribution system and are sold through traditional stores. Online retail sales, which include wine, have grown at ten times the rate of store sales. Keep in mind that many wineries have their own web sites, which are filled with specific and auxiliary information.

The Supreme Court Acts

In December 2004, a groundbreaking case went before the Supreme Court. At issue was the clash between the Twenty-first Amendment, which gives the states the right to regulate their own alcohol sales, and the Commerce Clause of the Constitution, which prohibits states from discriminating against out-of-state competitors. One of the reasons the Supreme Court will hear a case is to settle conflicting decisions by lower courts. In the domain of interstate wine shipping, two court decisions—one in Michigan and one in New York—came to opposite conclusions. Both states discriminated against out-of-state wineries in preference of in-state producers. The Michigan court ruled that Michigan's ban on direct shipping was permitted under the Twenty-first Amendment. The New York court ruled that the shipping ban was unconstitutional. Whatever way the Supreme Court rules, it will take some time for consumers to feel the effects of the changes.

In May 2005, the Supreme Court ruled that it's unconstitutional to grant preference to in-state wine shippers, opening the way for interstate shipment of wine. U.S. states must now allow shipment of wine from other states if they permit in-state wine shipments. But states that do not permit shipping wine at all may still continue to ban it.

The Big Boys Fight Back

Giant retailers like Wal-Mart and Costco have been able to offer their customers low prices in part because they negotiate large-volume buys directly from suppliers. Under the three-tier system in many states, the retailers can't buy from the producers and can't negotiate for lower prices.

Increasingly, the big-box retailers are looking to state courts for remedies, contending that state liquor regulations violate fair trade laws. Those retailers have a big stake in the outcome. While the court cases may take years to resolve, the decisions will affect what consumers ultimately pay for their wine.

Through the Grapevine

going right to the source

Of the 2,700 wineries in the United States, only 350 have output of more than 10,000 cases per year. The wines from large producers are the ones you see most often in the stores because they're the ones that the wholesalers buy. Small wineries with small production rely on direct sales to consumers.

Limited Production Means Higher Prices

No one will ever know why Beanie Babies became such a craze in the 1990s. Tiny stuffed toys that cost pennies to produce—and people were paying fortunes to get them. Clever marketing was certainly involved. As each Beanie Baby was "retired," a scarcity mentality kicked in, and prices went through the roof.

Scarcity in supply determines wine prices as well. Consider the so-called "cult" wines of Napa Valley—extreme examples, maybe. But these big, robust Cabernets with equally big reputations are made in such minuscule quantities that wine collectors are willing to pay incredible sums for them. It's a universal economic rule at work. When you have a small supply of a product, you can charge a higher price.

Look at single-vineyard wines. The quantity of wine that can be produced in a single vineyard in a single year is finite. When it's gone, it's gone. A winemaker can't go buy more grapes elsewhere. As a result, the price of a winery's single-vineyard wine will be more expensive than its others.

$OMMELIER CENTS

the parker effect

Legendary wine connoisseur Robert Parker has dominated the charts when it comes to assessing wines. Parker and other wine critics meet annually for a *primeur* tasting of wines, and when Parker changes his mind, his loyal followers go along with Parker, creating what vintners call "The Parker Effect"—exaggerated prices for a select number of wines and a lapse in demand for excellent wines that simply didn't make the cut. If you want to save money, let others buy into "The Parker Effect."

Thumbs Up!

Like with movies, a good review for a wine can drive demand. Retailers will tell you that every day of the week customers come into their stores holding a *Wine Spectator* score sheet or the most recent *Wall Street*

Journal "Tastings" column. High-profile experts have a lot of power in spurring sales of wines they endorse.

For a lot of folks, the guy next door has even more influence. Word of mouth is powerful—particularly when the mouth belongs to someone whose opinion you respect. Unlike the movies where the price at the ticket window stays the same regardless of a movie's ratings, a wine's popularity has an eventual effect on price.

If It Costs More, It Must Be Better?

Certainly, demand affects price. But it also works the other way around. Consider this revealing, perhaps apocryphal, story about Ernest Gallo, the founder of the giant American wine company. During his early years selling wine, he visited a New York buyer. He offered the buyer two samples of the same red wine. The buyer tasted the first one and asked about the price. Gallo told him it was five cents a bottle. The buyer tried the second wine and asked the price. This time Gallo said the wine cost ten cents a bottle. The buyer chose the ten-cent bottle. Sometimes, the more expensive the wine is, the more desirable it becomes. And, sometimes, the reverse is true.

Can It Be Done Cheaper?

In the late 1990s, the United States experienced a domestic grape shortage. In order to maximize their revenue, American producers concentrated on making wines that sold for over $14 a bottle. That left a giant opportunity in the low-priced wine market. An Australian company was poised to take advantage of that opportunity.

Back in 1957, Filippo and Maria Casella arrived in Australia from Sicily. After several years of cutting sugar cane and picking grapes, Filippo bought a forty-acre farm. In 1969, he started producing wine. For the next quarter of a century the Casellas made wine and lived in the small, one-story house nestled in their vineyards.

In 1994, Filippo turned the business over to his son John, who expanded the capacity of the winery. By the late '90s, the Casella winery was producing a low-priced, well-respected wine that, in its first year and a half, sold 19,000 cases.

$OMMELIER CENTS

two-buck chuck

During the California grape glut of 2000, Charles Shaw winery created a new category of American wines— Super Value Wines—and made an exclusive deal with Trader Joe's stores to carry its varietals at the rock bottom price of $1.99. Although it sent shockwaves through the wine industry, causing many producers to cry foul and even seek governmental reprieve, the wines proved so tasty and so *uber*-affordable that Trader Joe's couldn't restock them fast enough to keep up with consumer demand.

In January 2001, John took samples of his wine to a New York importer. The importer liked the easy-drinking, fruity taste and the $7 retail price, although he had reservations about the kangaroo on the label. Well, they immediately introduced the wine into the American market, and in the first seven months, the Yellow Tail brand sold 200,000 cases. The American wine-drinking public jumped on the bandwagon. Three years after its introduction, sales of Yellow Tail reached 7 million cases.

Hot Markets, Cool Prices

The early years of the new century brought with them an oversupply of grapes to the wine business.

Over-planting of vineyards in Northern and Central California led to a glut, and prices took a nosedive. It meant that producers could get inexpensive grapes and upgrade the quality of their wines at the same time. Similar to Yellow Tail's strategy, the domestic producers identified a price they would sell their wines for and tailored their production and marketing plans to make the price possible.

A number of these "market-driven" wines were introduced that combined above-average quality and prices in the $10 range. Some of these "hot" wines include the following:

- HRM Rex-Goliath Cabernet, Merlot, Pinot Noir, and Chardonnay: $8
- Castle Rock Winery Cabernet, Merlot, Pinot Noir, Syrah, Zinfandel, Chardonnay, and Sauvignon Blanc: $7 to $12
- Jewel Wine Collection in nine varietals: $10
- Three Thieves Zinfandel, Cabernet, Bianco in one-liter jugs: $7 to $10
- Jest Red blend: $10
- McManis Family Vineyards Cabernet, Merlot, Syrah, Chardonnay, and Pinot Grigio: $9 to $10

TIER THREE: THE RETAILER AND THE RESTAURANT

The tier-one folks (the producers) and the tier-two people (the wholesalers) have made the wine, packaged it, and delivered it to its selling destination—with their attendant markups. Now, it's on to tier three: your favorite restaurant or retail store.

Places that sell wine come in various forms. Depending on where you live, you can buy wine from a corner market, an exclusive wine shop, a supermarket, or a supersized discount warehouse. The similarity among the venues is an average markup of 50 percent over their cost—what the wholesaler charged them.

The other tier-three player is the restaurant. Three times the wholesale price is the standard markup when you buy a bottle to accompany your meal. The markups can vary among restaurants. A "white tablecloth" restaurant probably charges more than a neighborhood joint for the same bottle.

Markup variations occur also within a restaurant's own wine list. The least expensive bottles and the most expensive bottles may have higher markups than bottles in the midrange. Wines sold by the glass are marked up the most. While buying by the glass is a real convenience, you can be paying a four-time markup.

Now that you know what costs have gone into a bottle of wine, the choice is yours.

chapter 8

A CRASH COURSE ON $HOPPING FOR CHEAP WINE

. . . .

The world of wine changes every day. New vintages are released. New wineries spring up. Old grape varieties are rediscovered. As if those things aren't adjustments enough, the wine marketplace is going through its own dramatic changes. Do you buy bottles or boxes? Do you buy from a neighborhood wine store or stock up online? The savvy wine consumer explores all options.

. . . .

READY, SET, SHOP, AND SCORE!

Depending on where you live, your wine shopping options can be abundant—or severely restricted. With every state on its own to set rules for wine sales, consumers have unequal opportunities to buy wine. At one extreme are the states that control all aspects of wine sales—from choosing the wines to put on the shelves, to posting store hours, to employing the clerks who bag your purchases. At the other end of the spectrum are states that freely allow sales in locations like supermarkets, discount warehouses, convenience stores, drugstores, and gas stations in addition to traditional wine shops.

It All Starts with Knowledge!

The first thing you need to do is educate yourself! A knowledgeable wine buyer is an economical wine buyer. With the vast amount of information available on the Internet and in information-packed books and wine magazines, it's easy to jettison your wine education into overdrive. Here are some basic guidelines:

- Check out the excellent wine-related Web sites mentioned in this book and the list of great books in the appendix.
- Check out individual winery Web sites, which are chock full of valuable information.
- Read both wine specific and generic magazines that, along with local newspapers, frequently run feature articles on savvy wine buying and regularly run top ten lists of the best values.

Keep in mind that the more you read, the more you'll know, and the more you'll save!

Create a Budget

If you're a conscientious buyer, you already know not only how to construct a budget, but the vast benefits of doing so. Knock yourself out—make a plan! If you're not the kind of person who sits down and creates a budget, and you're pondering a sharp cutback, yet don't want to drive yourself mad with purchase-by-purchase decisions, consider the following generic suggestions for saving money spent on wine:

- At the very least, create a *philosophical* budget for wine and alcohol purchases. Do you consider wine an everyday expense, or do you consider wine a luxury item? Luxury items are limited to expenses above and beyond your needs.
- Always pay by cash or a debit card. Credit cards create a false reality. If you have to shell out cash, you're more likely to reconsider your purchase and make smarter decisions, avoiding impulse buys that you'll later regret.
- Always shop with a list and don't stray from it. Again, avoid impulse buys or being swayed by a promotional price on something you don't really want or need.
- Only shop once or twice a month. This will further eradicate impulse buys and will help you stay within the parameters of your budget.

After you've done your homework and amassed enough knowledge to make you a savvy buyer, it's time to hit the stores. Let's discuss your options.

WHERE TO BUY BARGAIN WINES

Wine specialty stores vary in size, selection, price points, and employee expertise. But they're the best place for the novice wine drinker to start. You have a good chance of finding someone knowledgeable about wine in general—and certainly knowledgeable about the store's inventory.

Rule Number One: Shop Around

When it comes to where you buy your wine, the key elements to consider are:

- Do they have a wide variety of prices?
- Do they have a substantial depth of selection?
- Do they offer a premiere level of service?
- Do they manage temperature control?

In pricier shops you'll find passionate and knowledgeable sales clerks, and, oddly enough, quite frequently a treasure trove of inexpensive wines. While independent wine shops will carry *la crème de la crème* of wine and champagne, they are also likely to stock a wider, better selection of affordable wines. Their buyers often forego high-paying careers to passionately pursue the best wine at the best price—they consider it their quest to find tasty wines at all price points, which means you reap the benefits.

Lower-priced "barns" frequently make their selections based on what the wineries want to clear out at bargain-basement prices. Expensive shops could actually end up saving you money without sacrificing taste.

Rule Number Two: Find an Ally

Shop in smaller retail outlets where you can build mutually beneficial relationships and then cultivate sales clerks as valuable resources. Not only are they well-versed in product, they're eager to build a repeat business. Tell them your price range and ask them to focus in on the best buys for your money. If they have a mailing list, make sure you sign up, and also ask to be notified when your favorites go on sale.

While you don't want to spend your bucks at gourmet markets, they are an excellent source for experimentation. Many wine experts at these types of stores spend their days sampling product. If you can latch onto their coat tails, definitely solicit their opinion. Tell them you adore Grigich Cellars, but you're hosting a large party and would like to buy something equally delicious, but a tad more economical. Often, they'll steer you to a wine that fits the bill perfectly. Also, ask about quantity discounts and foster an ongoing relationship. That way, the expert will become acquainted with your taste level and will alert you when they've got a fresh shipment coming in of something you're bound to love.

Through the Grapevine

keep an open mind

If you want to track down wines that were recommended in a newspaper or magazine, by all means take the article with you to the store. Just be forewarned that, with the millions of wine available, your store may not stock the exact wine recommended in the paper. The wine merchant should be able to easily come up with acceptable alternatives.

In an owner-operated store or one that has good staff training, the person behind the counter has likely tasted a lot of the wines the store carries. He/she can direct you to the types of wines you're looking for in your price category, suggest alternatives you might enjoy, or help you select a special-occasion or food-matched wine.

KNOWING WHAT'S IN STORE

When you want to explore the wine shelves on your own, it's helpful to know a few things common to most stores that will help your quest to find exceptional value wines.

Getting the Best Bargain

Before you hit the stores, stock up on these bargaining tips and you'll soon be saving mega bucks:

- Do your homework! Know as much about wines, wine regions, varietals, and prices as possible.
- Make smart buys according to your pre-thought-out plan (see "Building Your Caché" on page 138 for suggestions).
- Decide ahead of time how much you want to spend. And resist impulse buys.
- Shop at the stores that tend to price expensive wines at or below market; their prices are probably fair on low-priced wines.

Where to Find What

Wines are often organized by country of origin. For classic regions like France, wines may be organized into smaller regions like Bordeaux, Burgundy, and the Rhone. Red wines and whites may be in separate sections. Other times stores will organize their wines by varietal. There's usually a separate section for sparkling wines. Rare and expensive wines are often located in a specially designated area—and, occasionally, an entirely separate room.

At some point every store has to make room for new inventory and will put wines on sale. You'll often find them in special bins or boxes with case cards—large cardboard signs—describing the wines.

Is It Chilling or Grilling?

Take notice of a store's storage conditions. High heat and sunshine bearing down on their stash of wine have a deleterious effect. Any wines parked in the sunlight or in the heat aren't being treated well. Most better quality wine shops have temperature-controlled areas for storage. They will also have their wines (except, perhaps, mass market wines that move quickly) lying in a horizontal position.

Who's Doing the Talking?

You've undoubtedly noticed little cards taped to the store shelves that describe individual wines and tell you how well this wine "pairs beautifully with chicken" and that wine has a "lovely finish." They're "shelf talkers." Can you trust them? *Hmm.* Keep in mind that they're usually written by the wholesalers or the wineries that produced the wine—hardly objective sources.

As such, they're probably of limited value. Other times the retailer writes them. The store could be steering you toward a good wine with good value. Or the store may have bought a lot of the stuff and wants to move it. Still other shelf talkers give you numerical scores. The question to ask yourself is: Do I know and respect the person or publication awarding this score? If the answer is "no," don't let the score influence your purchase decision.

Through the Grapevine

label decoder

As with food items in general, rules about labeling are not always factual:

- "Bottled by" means someone else produced the wine.
- "Blended and bottled by" means the winery blended their own grapes.
- "Estate bottled' or "grown, produced, and bottled by" means the winery controlled all aspects of its production.
- "Stainless steel fermentation" or "no malolactic" generally indicates drier, more acidic qualities.
- "Buttery" or "oak fermentation" or "aging" usually indicates a richer, full-bodied wine. It may have been "aged" via insertion of oak chips.
- Residual sugar levels rising above .5 indicate a sweeter wine.

Can I Have a Sip?

If your state allows in-store wine tastings, it's the ideal scenario for buying. Sure, you're only getting a tiny little taste—and probably out of a little plastic cup at that. And, yes, it might be a wine that the store or wholesaler wants to push. But it's a whole lot better than buying blind. Even the big warehouse stores frequently have tastings sponsored by the various wineries or distributors. Make sure you get on their mailing list and attend free tastings regularly.

In areas where in-store tasting isn't possible, retailers often cosponsor wine tastings with restaurants. They're inexpensive ways to sample a variety of wines. And, of course, you know where to buy the wines afterward.

Can I Return This?

A reputable retailer will replace a bottle of wine if it's defective. Just shove the cork back in and take it back. It probably goes without saying that the bottle should be mostly full. Wine merchants who value their customers will often take back a bottle they've recommended if you're not happy with it. A happy customer is a repeat customer, but play your part by expressing your unhappiness tactfully. And don't make a habit of it.

DISCOUNT WAREHOUSES AND SUPERSTORES

Everybody needs cheap wine at some point. Make that "inexpensive" or—as the wine industry strongly prefers—a "good value" wine. Who isn't cost-conscious— particularly when you're buying in quantity? The discount warehouse is where you're going to find lower prices. These stores have truly strong purchasing power. They buy single brands of liquor by the trailer load, and when they call to place an order, their wholesalers jump.

Discount warehouses can buy for less and afford a lesser markup on their inventory (30 to 40 percent, rather than 50 to 60 percent) because of the volume of business they do. Some of the wines at these stores sell at prices below what the smaller stores pay wholesale for the same wines.

The downside of warehouse or superstore buying is you give up service and selection. It may be difficult to locate someone knowledgeable about the wines. And you don't have a big variety of wines to choose from. The wines are mainly large-production wines that can support the big advertising budgets that go into making them popular. Not that there's anything wrong with that! It's just that the superstores aren't the places to necessarily look for that special, limited production bottle.

Supermarkets account for 30 percent of U.S. wine sales. A combination of convenience and attractive pricing is pushing that number upward. Wine selection at supermarkets reflects the personality of the chain: mass market and highly advertised wines at mass retailers and more esoteric bottles at upscale markets. As consumers have become more savvy, more price conscious, and eager for exceptional values, private label wines have grown in favor. Some large grocery chains are introducing private label wines. Safeway, for example, carries private label wines that are often produced by known wineries and are very drinkable wines at exceptional prices.

HONING YOUR $HOPPING $KILLS

The more wine buying and wine tasting you do, the more you hone your skills for identifying a good deal. Whether you're a beginner trying to develop your tastes or a wine enthusiast searching for the "ultimate" bottle, the best basic advice is to get to know your retailer. He can give you more than recommendations. Once he knows your preferences, he can give you a heads-up about special arrivals and can give you advance notification of promotions and sales.

General Tips

Once you've ferreted out the best retailers, here are a few ideas to help you make the most of a growing relationship:

- Sign up for wine shop and winery mailing lists.
- Join *free* wine clubs so you can get limited edition wine at a fair price.
- Experiment with smaller, emerging-market, or start-up wineries to expand your repertoire.
- If you don't know the wine, sample it.
- Find a wine critic that speaks to your taste.
- Surf the Internet to preshop prices.

Start at the Beginning

With the millions of bottles you have to choose from, where do you start? You start small. First, become familiar with a certain grape. If you particularly like Sauvignon Blanc, start experimenting. Try Sauvignon Blanc from California. Try Sauvignon Blanc from New Zealand. Try Sauvignon Blanc from different wineries. And, if you get the chance, try them side by side. The differences—and similarities—become obvious.

Get to know a region. If the Cabernet you like is from Alexander Valley, California, try a different Cabernet from that same region. Look for similar tastes that might be due to the climate and soil . . . the *terroir*.

Find a producer you like and try its other wines. If you like the Chardonnay from Château Potelle, take a chance and buy a bottle of the Cabernet and the Zinfandel and the Sauvignon Blanc. The wines are different, but the winemaker and the philosophy of winemaking are the same.

Building Your Caché

Keeping your cellar stocked with a variety of wines will prevent last-minute buys that frequently lead to spending more than you would if you had a reserve on hand. Try the following list:

- Dry White: Sauvignon Blanc, Fumé Blanc, Pinot Grigio (or Pinot Gris)
- Full-bodied White: Chardonnay
- Sweet White: White Zinfandel, Riesling, Gewürztraminer
- Light Reds: Pinot Noir, Gamay Beaujolais
- Heavy Reds: Cabernet Sauvignon, Petite Sirah (or Shiraz), Barbera, Merlot, Zinfandel
- White Dessert: Muscat, Ice Wine, Botrytis
- Red Dessert: Port

DIVE IN: STRATEGIES FOR BUYING WINE

Maybe you've found a wine that you really like. It's comfortable. It's safe. You buy the same brand each time because you know what to expect. But there's a big world of wine out there. Experimentation, of course, has the potential to be both disappointing and expensive. But it's less of a risk when you have a strategy, so let's discuss some basics.

Avoid Trends

Just as clothing goes in and out of fashion, grapes do too. One varietal can be hot, hot, hot for a time . . . then recede somewhat in popularity as another takes its place.

When a varietal achieves a certain level of popularity, everyone starts to produce it to cash in on the craze.

The inevitable result is an influx of mediocre wines. Merlot was a perfect example. Ultimately, though, the fad chasers move on to other varietals. There will always be quality Merlots.

Popularity determines price. It starts in the vineyards, and it extends to the marketplace. Cabernet and Chardonnay are still among the big sellers with the price tags to match. You may want to steer clear of the most popular varietals, such as Chardonnay, Cabernet Sauvignon, Merlot, or at least THE brand at the moment, and anything else that everyone wants. They're often overpriced simply because everyone wants them. Being an individual is so much more fun!

So be a savvy buyer and cast a glance elsewhere for grape deals.

Some "Different" Wines to Sample

Red	White
Malbec	Chenin Blanc
Mourvèdre	Pinot Gris
Tempranillo	Gewürztraminer
Grenache	Viognier
Sangiovese	Pinot Blanc
Tempranillo	Grüner Veltliner
Carignan	Fiano
Carmenère	Albariño
Pinotage	

Go for Cheaper Real Estate

Napa, Bordeaux, Burgundy, Tuscany . . . now, you're talking big bucks. Other wine-producing regions around the world with less-expensive real estate frequently offer exceptional wine value. If France is your objective, get a bottle from Provence, the Loire Valley, or Languedoc-Roussillon. If you're in the mood for Italian, look for wine from Campania, Calabria, Puglia, or Sicily.

Spanish wines have become exceptionally popular—with prices inching up as a result. But you can still find bargains from regions other than Rioja: Galicia, Rueda, Navarra, Penedès, and Priorato. You can say the same thing about South American wines. Both Chile and Argentina still are great deals.

Load Up on Seconds

Wines that aren't quite up to snuff in quality to be bottled by a winery under its primary—and most prestigious—label may be bottled under a second label. It's not that the wine isn't any good. In fact, for wineries that have incredibly high standards, the rejected wine might be very, very good—indeed virtually indistinguishable from the prestigious label. Château Lafite is said to have started this practice in the eighteenth century, and other Bordeaux châteaus followed their example. In great vintage years, the gap between a winery's primary label and its second label is very narrow. Some second labels from famous Bordeaux chateaus include:

- Carruades de Lafite from Château Lafite Rothschild
- Pavillon Rouge from Château Margaux
- Haut-Bages-Averous from Château Lynch-Bages
- Château Bahans-Haut-Brion from Château Haut-Brion
- Marbuzet from Château Cos d'Estournel

The United States, including the Napa Valley, has its second labels too. When wineries had excess wine that they couldn't sell under their flagship brands, or wines that didn't quite reach muster, they created second labels. Again, even though the secondary label wine may be virtually indistinguishable from the primary brand, it sells for less, making it a real value to consumers. Some of those American second labels include the following:

- Liberty School from Caymus Vineyards
- Hawk Crest from Stags' Leap Wine Cellars
- Decoy from Duckhorn
- Glass Mountain from Markham
- Bonverre from St. Supery
- Tin Pony from Iron Horse
- Pritchard Hill from Chappellet
- Rubicon Estates from Francis Ford Coppola
- Bravura from Opus One
- Eshcol from Trefethen Vineyards

Wineries with big budgets have taken second labels in a slightly different marketing direction. Instead of relying on a surplus of wine, they produce wines specifically targeted to the budget-minded. They blend wines from different regions that they can sell at low prices. Beringer produces Napa Ridge. Mondavi produces Woodbridge. Sebastiani produces Talus. And Fetzer produces Bel Arbor.

Gamble on Good Years

Some years are safer than others to gamble on unknown producers. If a region has experienced a terrific vintage year, the wines from the major producers can get out of sight. But the smaller, lesser-known producers have produced wines under the same climatic conditions. The year 2000, for example, is considered an outstanding vintage in Bordeaux. Any 2000 Bordeaux will likely be pretty good.

what's hot in 2006 bargains!
California Chenin Blanc, German and California Rieslings, Australian Shiraz, Sauvignon Blanc from New Zealand (or anywhere), and full-bodied red wines from France's over-stocked Rhone Valley are all great buys for 2006.

Stock Up During Sales

When a store is making room for new inventory and puts the "old" bottles on sale, you could run into some treasures. And in larger stores, they might be discounting whole cases. This is a bargain-hunter's paradise. Because you may not be able to tell at a glance which bottles are treasures and which ones are trash, it's prudent to buy just one and try it out first before investing in more.

When you find promotional prices on your favorites, definitely stock up. The best months for bulk buys: January, when retailers are anxious to clear out excess holiday inventory; and August, when merchants want to clear out old inventory to make room for new wines.

Buy by the Case

Most retailers offer case discounts. You can mix and match and fill the twelve bottle slots with different wines if you want. The usual discount is 10 percent, but some will go as high as 15 percent, particularly for repeat customers. Some wine merchants discount further if you buy a case of the same wine. You don't need to have an elaborate wine cellar to take advantage of case savings. It just makes sense if you buy wine on a regular basis. A few hot tips for case buying:

- To maximize bulk buys, form buyer co-ops with your friends and family.

- Ask the retailer if you can pay cash and receive a discount—saving them the cost of credit card usage.
- Ask the retailer if he's willing to offer an additional discount on hard liquor. To win your repeat business, they may well allow you to score some premiere vodka at a bargain price.
- If they offer a mixed-case discount, select six affordable ($10 and under) wines, and splurge on six slightly higher-priced wines.

$OMMELIER CENTS

insider tip
The wineries call the months of October, November, and December "OND" and equate them with price slashing to unload excess inventory. Ask you favorite retailers what they've been savvy enough to score at rock-bottom prices and maybe they'll let you in on the cost savings.

DO SCREW TOPS = CHEAP WINE?

It wasn't all that long ago that the click, click, click of a screw top instead of the pop of a cork meant someone was opening a bottle of cheap swill. My, how times have changed. With tainted corks ruining so many wines—disappointing consumers and costing winemakers millions in the process—it was time someone found an alternative. And there it was, right under everyone's noses. But the cork is sacred to many wine drinkers who enjoy the theater of opening the bottle. So winemakers looking for cork replacements turned first to cork look-alikes.

Plastic Corks

You've, no doubt, run into a plastic cork by now. Some may have looked, at first glance, like a real cork. Some producers wanted to win over cork traditionalists. But most have very un-corklike colors: red, purple, yellow, black. Synthetic corks are made from either medical- or food-grade plastic. They're designed to be inert—so they don't affect the taste of the wine—and seal the bottle efficiently so no air gets in to spoil the wine.

Wines in plastic-stoppered bottles tend to age faster—so you're not apt to see them in wines that require years of aging. Plastic corks are better suited to wines intended for early drinking.

Through the Grapevine

bring on the frizz

Get out your "church-key" for these drink-me-now sparklers. Unlike other sparkling wines that keep the bubbles locked up with corks, Il Prosecco and Il Moscato from Mionetto Wines are topped with a crown cap. They're lightly sparking—*frizzante,* in Italian—and low in alcohol. And they're meant to be enjoyed right away.

The Stelvin Closure

The screw tops on wine bottles aren't the same ones you find on bottles of Miller Lite. After all, this *is* wine! In the 1950s, a French manufacturer developed the Stelvin screw top used on today's wine bottles. When it was first introduced in the '70s, it was a complete marketing disaster because the public perception was that the wine inside was cheap and inferior.

In the '90s, wineries in Australia and New Zealand adopted the Stelvin closure. It was a hit in their countries. In those days you could often buy an Aussie wine in the United States that had a cork . . . but the bottle had grooves at the mouth that were used back home for a twist-off cap. American wine enthusiasts, it was thought, would never adapt to screw tops. Then in 1997, screw tops got a lot of publicity when Gordon Getty, the owner of Napa's boutique PlumpJack Winery, announced he was going to use the twist-offs for his $150-a-bottle Cabernets.

Many other well-respected wineries have followed suit. Economics play a part because screw caps cost significantly less than corks. But the real issue is protecting the wine. And this time the wine-drinking public seems willing to accept the cork replacement. The tide toward alternative closures may have turned. There is some concern about the Stelvin's performance in long-term aging. But, so far, taste tests are generating optimism. And, with no necessity to keep the cork moist, you can store the bottles upright.

Some "Screwy" Recommendations:

- Bonny Doon Ca'del Solo Big House Red and Big House White: $10
- Argyle Winery Merlot: $30
- Screw Kappa Napa: $13
- R. H. Phillips Shiraz: $16

FOXY BOX WINE

It used to be that beer-drinking party animals who thought they were doing their wine-drinking friends a favor bought wine in boxes. The wine was . . . well, not the best. But, with a five-liter capacity, there was a lot of wine inside the box. If you wanted to keep it for weeks, you could. And it wouldn't deteriorate into anything worse.

wine in a bag?

The wine inside the box is actually contained in a vacuum-sealed plastic bladder. When the wine is dispensed through the attached tap, no air is allowed back in. And the plastic bag collapses. Without air contact to cause damage, the wine will stay fresher longer—a few weeks compared to a couple of days in a bottle. Longer drinkability means less waste!

Considering that the bag-in-a-box system works so well to preserve open wine, it's ironic that it has been used primarily for low-grade wines—until recently! Some producers have put their premium wines into boxes, and the packaging—once thought to be gauche—is gaining respect. And it has a new, foxy name: cask wine.

There have been a few changes. The box is smaller. Keep in mind that the popular three-liter box holds the equivalent of four bottles! And the technology for the valve system has been improved. It all makes sense: You can buy more wine for less money; the box is more portable and more easily stored than a bottle; and you can drink as little or as much at a time without oxidizing the wine.

The bag inside the box was invented in the 1950s as a container for battery acid. It caught on as a way to sell wine in Australia—where 55 percent of all wine is consumed in three-liter boxes. Now it's catching on in the United States. Wines that have received top ratings and won medals are going into boxes. A few of the new wines available in a box (remember 3 liters = 4 bottles):

- Black Box Chardonnay, Merlot, Cabernet Sauvignon, Shiraz: $25 (3 liters)
- Delicato Shiraz, Merlot, Chardonnay, Cabernet Sauvignon: $18 (3 liters)
- Jean-Marc Brocard Chablis Jurassique: $40 (3 liters)
- Banrock Station Chardonnay, Merlot, Cabernet Sauvignon, Shiraz: $16 (3 liters)
- Hardys Chardonnay, Merlot, Cabernet Sauvignon, Shiraz: $16 (3 liters)

Through the Grapevine

wine in a can!

Guess what—it's here! Sofia Blanc de Blanc, a sparkling wine in a bold, pink single-serving can, is sold in a four-pack—straws included. It's named after Sofia Coppola, daughter of film director Francis Ford Coppola, who just happens to own the winery.

BUYING WINE ONLINE

The Internet has opened up a worldwide marketplace for products. You can buy a sarong, a garage door opener, and a slab of granite with the click of a mouse. But because wine is a highly regulated product, it's not quite as simple to order it online. If you've already tried making a Web wine purchase, you've noticed that one of the first questions you're asked is where you live. Your state determines whether wine can be shipped to you.

For those U.S. residents who are permitted to ship wine into their states, the Internet is a virtual wine cellar. Selection is almost limitless. No longer confined just to brick-and-mortar stores, wine drinkers can purchase wines directly from their favorite producers or compare prices right at their keyboard.

After the dust settled from the dot-com crashes of the '90s, the online Web merchants who survived came back stronger. And new ones emerged. Today, you can buy wine from Internet-only sellers, from wineries, from traditional retailers, and from individuals.

Even with all the restrictions, online wine sales have risen.

It's possible to search for wine by region, type of wine, vintage year, price, producer, and name. And when you do, you'll get information about ratings, awards, suppliers, winemakers, release dates, latest news—among hundreds of other tidbits. Still, the Internet will never completely replace your local merchant. There's still the need to examine, touch, discuss . . . and drink it tonight!

KNOW THYSELF AND THY WINE

If you drink wine, and you want to save money, it's crucial to remember whether or not you liked it. The good wine experiences you want to repeat . . . the bad ones you want to avoid. If you're like most people, you think you can remember what you liked and didn't like without writing anything down. This system doesn't work. If you write one sentence about each wine you try, you'll learn what your preferences are and avoid unnecessary disappointments and clumsy purchases.

If all varietals were created equal, remembering what you enjoyed wouldn't be so tough. But not all Chardonnays are the same, and no two Merlots taste alike. What happens to a lot of people is that they drink a bottle of a certain type of wine they like—maybe an Australian Shiraz—and they think they've found the red wine for them. They may, over time, come to realize that they really only like one Shiraz out of every three or four they try. Without record keeping, it may take a while to figure this out. Worst of all, it's easy to forget which ones you actually liked.

A Wine Journal

By keeping track of the wines you consume, you'll discover more than what wines you enjoy. You'll get a visual idea of the wines you've missed that you need to try. Here's some vital information to include in your journal:

- Name of the wine
- Name of the producer
- Country and region
- Vintage year—if it has one
- Price
- Where and when you tasted it (and with whom)
- Food you ate with it
- Color
- Aroma
- Taste
- Any other comments that may help you remember the wine later

One of the most helpful visual elements in remembering a wine is the label. Removing it can be frustrating, but there are products on the market that can simplify the task. One popular label removal system is a large adhesive strip that you lay over the label and then pull away from the bottle. It splits the wine label and removes only the printed surface, which you can adhere to the page of your journal.

Getting the label off without such aids can be a snap—or it can be problematic, depending on the adhesive the bottler uses. To test, use a razor to take up the corner of the back label. If the back of the label is sticky, fill the empty bottle with the hottest water you can and let it stand for a few minutes. Test the back label again by sliding the razor under the label to start it. It should peel right off.

If the back of the label isn't sticky, you've got more work to do. After you've filled the bottle with hot water, submerge the whole bottle into more hot water and let it soak for a few minutes up to a few hours. Then try removing the label, starting the process with the razor. Some people have more success when they add soap or ammonia to the soaking water. Good luck! The process might be more fun with a little wine.

QUICK TIPS TO WRAP UP

Here are a few quick tips for helping you score real bargains:

- Experiment!
- Educate yourself.
- Make friends at retail shops.
- Join wine tasting groups.
- Keep a wine tasting journal.
- Buy lower-priced varietals.
- Buy from smaller, lesser-known regions.
- Try boxed wines for everyday use or parties.
- Check out warehouse or superstore specials.
- Form your own personal buying co-op.

chapter 9

ORDERING WINE AT A RESTAURANT WITHOUT $PENDING A FORTUNE

. . . .

How many articulate, high-powered executives have been reduced to indecisive, gutless wimps when handed a restaurant wine list? Plenty! But that's not your style. Sure, choosing the perfect wine match may be intimidating. Sure, you've got a spending limit on your Visa card. Sure, all eyes are on you. But by the time you finish this chapter, you'll know what to order when, how to order it with confidence, and how to do it within your budget.

. . . .

MR. CHEAP

RESTAURANT BASICS

All restaurants have their own "attitude." And you see their attitude in everything they do from the time they take your phone reservation to the moment they hand you the check. When it comes to wine, their attitude is just as obvious.

The Wine List

The first clue to a restaurant's wine personality—and to the kind of wine experience you're likely to have—is the "list." It can be as simple as a glass of red, a glass of white, and a glass of pink. No one is saying this is good or bad or right or wrong. You merely adjust your expectations accordingly. If you happen to be in a small ethnic restaurant offering some *vino bianco* from the homeland, this could be a wine night to remember.

At the other restaurant extreme, you might be handed a list with thousands of wines that requires weight training just to lift. The upside is that the establishment clearly has an interest in wine, and you can't help but find *something* to drink. The downside is too many pages and too little time.

A restaurant reveals its attitude not only by the number of wines it offers. Selection is another key. Some lists will give you household names—highly advertised, popular, everyday wines. Who could object to that? You know what you're getting: comfort and dependability. But where's the excitement?

Restaurants that really care about their customer's wine experience will offer a varied selection—some familiar names, some unknown—regardless of list size. You can decide for yourself whether you're in the mood for something tried-and-true or ready for an adventure.

The Server

Who presented the wine list to you? Was it your waiter or a sommelier? The sommelier is the restaurant's wine specialist (and not all restaurants have one) who creates the wine list and often serves the wine. Any restaurant with a sommelier (usually high-end places) cares about wine. Sommeliers have a reputation for being snooty. In reality, that's rarely the case. They're knowledgeable, well-trained professionals who can guide your wine selection based on preferences, food pairings, and price. Chances are, a sommelier will make your decision-making effortless.

Without a sommelier, next in line to answer your wine questions is the waiter. That can be a mixed bag. If well trained, the server will be acquainted enough with the wines to describe to you how they taste. If not . . . well, you're on your own.

Even if your server isn't equipped to provide a knowledgeable recommendation, he reflects the wine attitude of the restaurant in other ways. He may or may not be trained to present and pour according to long-standing wine traditions. He may or may not be attentive to you when your glass is empty. Or he may be overzealous in pouring by prematurely topping off the glasses so you run out of wine before your entrée is served—necessitating another bottle, of course.

Their Glassware

If you went to a restaurant and ordered a $30 steak and then got plastic utensils to eat it with, you'd be plenty mad. But that's the kind of treatment most of us have come to accept when we order wine: a pricey Cabernet served in cheap glasses.

The typical glassware is either too small or too thick. Sometimes the glasses have no stems—which may be acceptable for a theme restaurant—but an eatery that makes wine a priority shows its wine-drinking customers respect by using appropriate glasses.

DECIPHERING THE WINE LIST

How wines are presented and described on the list can be helpful in your decision-making—or not. There's no way of predicting what you'll find—except, of course, for the prices. Wine lists come in all shapes, sizes, degree of description, and degree of accuracy.

Basic Classifications

Most often, wines will be listed under general headings of red, white, sparkling, and dessert. This presentation is limited in its usefulness. But it does come in handy for unfamiliar Old World wines—the ones that are named after geographical locations with no mention of grape variety. Like Château Canon La Gaffeliere Saint-Emilion. (It's red.) Or for varietal wines made from grapes you've never heard of. Like Lemberger. (It's red, too.)

This generic-type wine list will occasionally include after-dinner drinks in its dessert wine section. So, in addition to Sauternes and Ports, you may find liqueurs and single-malt Scotches.

Listing by Country or Varietal

More detailed lists may be subdivided by country, region, or varietal. In this scenario, wines might be listed under French Reds, Italian Reds, and American Reds or specified further by Bordeaux, Campania, and California. With varietal listings, likely headings in the white wine section are Chardonnay, Sauvignon Blanc, and Pinot Grigio.

"Stylish" Wine Lists

Words like *big*, *full-bodied*, *fresh*, *oaky*, and *dry* may be more meaningful than geographical and varietal headings to someone not acquainted with a particular wine. And that's why a lot of wine lists are organized according to their style. Under a white heading of "Dry and Crisp," you could find a Pinot Grigio alongside a Sancerre and Chablis. A short but descriptive "Big Reds" might include a California Cabernet and an Italian Barolo. When you have no clue about a wine's grape heritage or region of origin, you'll get the general idea of taste from this sort of listing.

$OMMELIER CENTS

how much do i order for a group?

To err on the side of being frugal, avoid ordering too much wine at the outset. The rule of thumb is about a half bottle per person—although that could go way up or down according to your group's drinking profile. For a group of three or more whose wine preferences you don't know, it's always safe to order both a red and a white. But no matter which varietals you choose, always start low and only order more if your guests are clamoring for it.

Progressive Lists

Some lists will put wines in some sort of progressive sequence—like from lightest in style to richest. In such a list you could expect to see a Beaujolais at or near the top, perhaps a Chianti in the middle, and a Cabernet at the end. Another "progressive" technique is listing the wines by price—either cheapest to most expensive or the reverse. This is helpful to the cost conscious and the status conscious. Really—who wants to be seen ordering the cheapest wine when it's so glaringly listed at the top?

STRATEGIES FOR CHOOSING A WINE

When was the last time your restaurant meal was ruined by a bad wine selection? Probably never. Sure, some matches may not have been exactly ethereal, but, chances are, you were able to enjoy the meal anyway. In the worst case, you might have had to "enjoy" the food and wine separately. So, first piece of advice: Don't sweat it. Now . . . on to specific strategies.

Strategy #1: Keep It "Friendly"

Certain wines are known to be food-friendly. For whatever reason, they can pair equally well with pompano and peanuts. It only makes sense, at a restaurant when everyone at the table will be ordering something different, to choose a wine that will go with everything.

Among the food-friendly wines are Pinot Noir and Riesling. One red, one white. That's all you have to remember. How easy can you get? The group wants red? Order a Pinot Noir. You'll find terrific Pinots from Oregon and California. And, of course, the Burgundy region of France. The group prefers white? Try an exceptional Riesling from upstate New York, Canada, Germany, or Alsace.

riesling conundrum

Ordering a Riesling has challenges. Rieslings range in overall character from bone-dry to super sweet. Dry Rieslings can usually be identified by "dry" on American labels and "trocken" on German labels. Rieslings are sometimes listed with other names. Johannisberg Riesling, Rhine Riesling, and White Riesling are all "real" Rieslings. Riesling Italico and Riesling-Sylvaner are different grapes altogether.

Strategy #2: Get a Sneak Preview

The one sure-fire way to choose a wine with confidence and impress your dining partners with your knowledge and sophistication is to have an advance copy of the wine list to study. In the quiet and comfort of your own home, you can decide what varietal, what winery, what vintage, and what price are best. And you can also learn to pronounce Pouilly-Fuissé (poo-yee-fwee-SAY).

A lot of restaurants today have Web sites—and a good share of those have their wine lists (in whole or in part) available there. The next option is a fax. Most restaurants will be pleased to send you the list, provided you're not calling them during their peak business hours. And the old-fashioned way still works: Make an in-person visit a day or two ahead of your reservation.

Strategy #3: Ask for Help!

There's no shame in asking for help. In fact, it shows a good deal of self-assurance. The person to ask is the sommelier.

If you're imagining the sommelier is a seventy-year-old tuxedoed Frenchman looking down his nose at you, you're behind the times. Today's sommeliers are often younger, hipper, and just as likely to be a woman as a man.

They're more like tour guides than professors. They'll ask you a bunch of questions about the kinds and styles of wines you like, what you might be ordering to eat, how open you are to try something new and different. And during your conversation, the sommelier will probably get a feeling for how much you plan to drink and how much you want to spend.

Sommeliers know their wine lists intimately . . . because, in most cases, they've created them. They have chosen the wines, negotiated the purchases, overseen the storage, written the descriptions, and trained the staff to serve the wines. Sommeliers are enthusiastic about sharing their wine finds. Sometimes they've been able to buy bottles that aren't available in any retail store. This could be your night to sip something truly remarkable.

WINE BY THE GLASS

What a concept! Wine by the glass has made it so easy—and relatively inexpensive—to throw caution to the wind and experiment with new and unfamiliar wines. But watch how a restaurant treats its opened bottles.

As soon as a bottle is uncorked, the wine begins to deteriorate because of contact with the air. So proper storage is paramount. There's a big difference in attitude between a restaurant that has an expensive preservation system that keeps wine fresh and a restaurant that's content to leave an opened bottle sitting on a counter until tomorrow's lunch crowd charges through the door. Of course, there's ample room in between these extremes for careful handling of opened wine.

$OMMELIER CENTS

sample test drive

Before you select a bottle or a wine by the glass and risk wasting money, ask your server if they already have bottles opened that you could sample. If so, they are usually willing to give you a "taste" before you buy. The restaurant seeks to please a customer, offering you the chance to either confirm your first choice or change your mind.

When you order a wine by the glass, it's perfectly acceptable to ask your server when the bottle was uncorked. If the wine has been hanging around for a day or two, you might be well served to make another selection.

WINE ETIQUETTE

For a beverage that dates back thousands of years, you'd expect there would be some traditions that go along with its consumption. Nowhere is that more obvious than inside a restaurant.

Presentation of the Cork

Way back when before wine bottles had labels, there was no real proof that a particular bottle of wine came from the winery it was attributed to. Human nature being what it is, some unscrupulous restaurateurs would pass off common French wine as having come from the famous châteaus. To maintain their good reputations, the châteaus began branding their corks. And restaurants began presenting them to customers to verify the wine's origin.

The practice continues to this day long after the need to do so has passed. So, what are you, the diner, supposed to do with the cork once the waiter has plopped it down in front of you? Anything you want. Ignore it. Examine it if you prefer. Sniff it if you feel like it. Slip it into your pocket to take as a souvenir. The cork won't tell you anything that won't be evident in the glass.

Presentation of the cork will become less of an issue as more and more wineries opt for screw top closures. Unless there's a winning sweepstakes number inside the cap, the screw top probably won't be presented for inspection.

Through the Grapevine

follow the clues

Corks that are either dry and crumbly or completely wet are a clue that air may have crept into the bottle and spoiled the wine. A taste will tell you. Occasionally, harmless tartrate crystals form at the end of the cork that had contact with the wine. They have no effect on taste.

The Tasting Ritual

You've seen the wine tasting dance dozens—if not hundreds—of times. It's virtually the *pas de deux* of wine server and wine sampler. What's all the fancy footwork about? Back in the days before modern winemaking methods, wine would often go bad—so patrons were offered the opportunity to sample their wine before drinking it. That's still the reason for the ritual. It's not merely to see if the wine meets your expectations. It's not to test your wine knowledge and show you up as a rube. It's simply to make sure you're getting the wine you ordered and that the wine is in good condition.

Here are the steps in the routine:

- The waiter presents the bottle for you to visually inspect. You check that it's the same wine and same vintage that you ordered. If not, speak up. If the wine you ordered isn't available, your server should make a recommendation for a similar wine *in the same price range.*
- The waiter cuts the capsule and removes the cork. He puts the cork on the table in front of you. You've already mastered this step.
- The waiter pours an itsy-bitsy, teeny-weeny bit of wine into your glass. You admire it. Study the wine against a white or light background— like the tablecloth or napkin.
- If the wine's color and clarity have met with your approval, it's time to swirl. Really get that wine moving around the glass. Now stick your nose right into the glass . . . and breathe deeply. *Ahh!*
- Assuming the aromas have been pleasing, take a sip. Hold the wine in your mouth. Roll it around on your tongue before you swallow.
- Now to the big finish. The wine is acceptable, and you nod to the waiter. That's his signal to pour for the group.
- That's all there is to it. Take a bow.

Sending a Wine Back

Whew! You took a whiff of the wine. No fruitiness there. It smelled more like a damp basement. You tasted it. You know there's something wrong. It's time to send the bottle back.

"I'm afraid this is a bad bottle, and I'd like to send it back." That's all you have to say. A waiter who knows wine will probably smell it for himself and cart off the offending bottle. He'll return with a replacement. Even if you're the only one who perceives the flaw, the waiter will most likely replace the wine anyway.

You don't have to feel bad that it's a financial hardship for the restaurant. The restaurant will, in turn, send the bottle back to the distributor for replacement.

Sample Before You Order

The tasting ritual is all about the condition of the wine—not just whether or not you're happy with your selection. But wouldn't it be nice to know ahead of time that you were going to like the wine you ordered?

A restaurant isn't about to open a bottle of wine just for you to taste. It would be too wasteful—and expensive—if you didn't like it. But if the bottle you're considering is also available by the glass, it's a different story. In that case, your waiter will likely be very willing to give you a small sample to try. And if he doesn't, you can always buy a glass to try. Then again . . . there's something very bold about venturing into the unknown.

BYO RESTAURANTS

Some of the best restaurants for enjoying wine have no wine lists at all. That's because you "Bring Your Own." You can pick out something special from your cellar or stop at a wine shop on the way and pick up something from the closeout shelf. You don't pay restaurant markups at BYOs. But you can expect to pay a corkage fee—for wine service and use of the restaurant's glassware. The fee is usually a per-bottle charge and can vary dramatically.

byo quick tips

If you prefer bringing your own bottle to restaurants here are a few quick tips:

- Sommeliers prefer selling you expensive bottles of wine and will wince less if you tell them ahead of time that your bargain wine has a special meaning.
- To save vast amounts of money, seek out new restaurants that don't yet have a liquor license; they're thrilled to have your business and are, therefore, more likely to dispense with corkage fees.
- If your dinner party is sufficiently large, you may get around multiple corkage fees by taking along a magnum or two. The restaurant might not charge you two corkage fees per magnum.

Wine enthusiasts with extensive collections and individuals who just have a special bottle will, occasionally, want to drink their wines at a restaurant over dinner. Restaurants with wine lists who permit this form of BYO obviously lose out on a wine sale. That's why they charge high corkage fees.

There are some rules of etiquette to follow when you want to take a bottle to a wine-serving restaurant. Never take a bottle that is already on the restaurant's wine list. Call in advance to check. In fact, calling ahead is always a good idea. When you explain that you've been saving this special wine for ten years to drink in celebration of your tenth anniversary, what restaurateur won't be charmed?

At tipping time, don't forget to do the right thing: Tip your waiter according to what the bill would have been had you ordered the wine from the restaurant's list.

GETTING THE MOST FOR YOUR MONEY

Let's face it—money is often a top priority when you choose a wine. If you had unlimited financial resources, you could order anything that struck your fancy. And if you didn't care for it—what the heck, you could order something else. Time for a reality check. The goal is to get the best possible wine for the dollars you plan to spend—in other words, the best value for your money.

$OMMELIER CENTS

while wolfgang fiddles, money burns

Mozart made you do it . . . spend more on wine, that is. A British study has shown that when restaurants play classical music, their customers buy pricier wines. Apparently, Beethoven, Mahler, and Vivaldi make people feel more sophisticated and more willing to pay for the pleasures of the grape.

How Restaurants Price Wines

Pricing policies are as different as the restaurants themselves. But here's a general rule of thumb. If the wholesale price of a bottle of wine is $10, a retail wine shop will charge $15. A typical restaurant will charge $20 to $30 for the same bottle.

The markups vary from wine to wine—the biggest markups being at the low and high ends of the list. At the low end, the wines are cash cows. Some customers want their wine and they want it cheap—and they're not too picky about what they get. And the restaurant makes a killing.

take flight!

Flights of wine are small tastes of wine (about two ounces apiece) served by a restaurant as a series. The four-to-six offerings are often based on a theme—Italian reds, for example, or whites with oak or wines with funny names. The purpose is to present wine lovers an opportunity to experiment with new wines at a reasonable cost.

At the other end of the list, you have a different scenario. The restaurant is selling either to the extremely well-heeled or to expense account diners who are indifferent to what the wine costs. Ka-ching! At the middle of the list, the wines usually have lower markups. And that's where you'll find the best value.

Some restaurants—especially those committed to the wine drinking public—have another approach. Their objective is to get their customers to drink more and higher-quality wines, and they achieve this through a pricing strategy of adding about $10 to the retail price of the wine. Even with these modest markups, the restaurant still makes money—and attracts faithful customers.

More Tips for the Value-Conscious

No one wants to be regarded as a cheapskate. But common sense says that if you maximize "value," you can order more bottles for less money. Here are some ways to do that:

- **Unless you're familiar with the "house" wine, skip it in favor of something else**. The restaurant probably bought it on the basis of price and gave it the highest markup.

- **Buy by the bottle.** A standard bottle contains four to six glasses of wine—depending on the size of the pour. Once you've purchased three wines by the glass, you've paid for a whole bottle.

- **Choose a wine from the same region as the restaurant's food specialty.** A good Italian restaurant, for example, will have a creative—and usually value-priced—selection of Italian wines.

- **Look for varietals that aren't all the current rage**. Chardonnays, Cabernets, and Merlots have been hot sellers in the past and have commanded higher dollars. Cast your eyes elsewhere for, say, Chenin Blanc or Pinot Gris or Malbec.

- **Experiment with wines from parts of the world where the land itself is less expensive (and, hence, the end cost of the wine is less expensive), like South America.**

chapter 10

$HOW TIME: ENTERTAINING AT HOME WITH PANACHE

. . . .

Wine is certainly an everyday beverage. But it can take on a special significance when you're entertaining. The wine you choose and the way you serve it sends a message to your guests. That doesn't mean exorbitantly expensive wines and pompous presentation. It means matching the wines to your friends and to the occasion—casual and formal alike—and taking care to show the wines at their best.

. . . .

KNOW THYSELF

Some men wouldn't be caught dead in a suit. Some women would never even consider going without pantyhose. Just as people have personal styles in dressing—some formal, some casual—they also have style preferences for entertaining. The great thing about wine is that it goes with all styles.

Your personality has a lot to do with the kinds of entertaining you're likely to enjoy. Consider whether you:

- Are outgoing—or more reserved.
- Don't mind being the center of attention—or prefer the periphery.
- Like to have detailed plans—or enjoy being "free-form."
- Are budget-minded—or don't have to worry about such things.
- Are label-conscious—or oblivious.

Look to your personality traits when you're planning to entertain at home. You want to be able to enjoy your own party—so choose a form of entertaining that you're comfortable with. That's not to say that you shouldn't stretch outside your comfort zone. But even if you're about to have a kind of party you've never hosted before (like a wine tasting!), you have a variety of ways to make the event fit your style.

How would you describe the parties you like going to? Small, intimate dinner parties? Outdoor barbecues? Body-to-body cocktail receptions? Family get-togethers? Poolside festivities? Whatever the activities—whether the event is indoors or out, or large or small—there's always the opportunity to bump up the celebration with wine.

GLASSWARE BASICS

It's safe to assume that every wine drinker—regardless of snob level, income level, or age—has drunk (and enjoyed) wine out of a plastic glass. Was it their first choice? Hardly. But it proves that an imperfect vessel isn't going to completely ruin a wine. It may not show the wine at its best, but you know what they say: any port in a storm.

When you entertain in your own home, you have choices. One of them is what glassware to use for serving wine. Yes, *glass*ware. Glass, unlike plastic, is inert and doesn't affect the taste of the wine. Consider the following guidelines for wine glass presentation:

- **Keep It Clean**—You might think that goes without saying, but there are all sorts of lingering "contaminants" that can make a wine taste off. Even if you've done your best in washing the glass but haven't rinsed it well, it will have detergent residue. If you've dried it with a dirty dishtowel, it'll have the telltale odor. Even dust will affect the wine's taste.

- **Stick with Clear**—Most wine enthusiasts will tell you it's important to see the wine—to check its clarity, to determine its age, or to just admire the color. A colored glass will not let you do any of those.

- **Opt for Thin**—Glasses with rolled rims can make the wine dribble into your mouth. A thin glass will present less foreign matter to come between you and the wine.

- **Go for Stemmed**—The stem allows you to not hold the bowl of the glass in your warm hand and, by contact, warm the wine.

- **Make It Tapered**—The bowl should narrow at the rim. It'll keep you from spilling when you swirl. And it will capture the aromas and not let them evaporate before you get your nose to the glass to sniff.

Buying Wineglasses

Do you need a different wineglass for each kind of wine? No. Do you want a different glass for each wine? Only you can answer that. It certainly depends on your interest, your budget, and your storage space. If you're just starting a glassware collection, it's helpful to know which ones to buy first, second, and third. This is a logical approach to purchasing stemware:

1. Start out with a **twelve-ounce glass**. You might think that sounds pretty big considering that a typical serving of wine is four to five ounces. But you want to leave plenty of room for swirling. You can use this as an all-purpose glass for either red or white wine.

2. A **Champagne flute** should be next on the list. Champagnes are the only wines that shouldn't be served from an all-purpose glass. The flute is tulip-shaped to keep the effervescence contained. The sherbet-style glasses let the bubbles dissipate too quickly.

3. Now it's time for another **all-purpose glass**— either larger or smaller. It depends on whether you want to use it for red wines (which traditionally are served in the larger glass) or for white wines. This decision will depend on your personal preference. If you want to choose whatever is in fashion, go with bigger.

4. Especially if you enjoy dessert wines and fortified wines, your next purchase should be a **copita**. It looks like a miniature version of the Champagne flute. The average serving size of a dessert wine is two to three ounces—so a smaller glass is called for.

CORKSCREWING AROUND

Even though wine producers are increasingly turning to screw tops instead of corks as closures for the bottles, corks are still the traditional closure—and will probably be around for some time to come. So if you're going to drink wine at home, you'll need a corkscrew. There are hundreds—maybe thousands—of corkscrews available. But they fall into some general categories.

From the low-tech end of the spectrum are the "pullers." You probably have one in a drawer that some company gave you instead of a pen with the company logo on it. They take the form of a T-shape with a handle and a worm. And there are no moving parts—which is why it depends on sheer force (yours) to get the cork out of the bottle.

The two-pronged puller requires less force but more finesse. It has no worm but two blades that you wedge into the bottle to grip the sides of the cork and pull. Professionals like it particularly for older corks that are in danger of crumbling. It's known as the "Ah-So." And it takes some practice to use.

Lever-type corkscrews can take a variety of forms from something you can put in your pocket to something you can mount on the wall. The most ubiquitous lever type is the butterfly corkscrew. It has a worm and butterfly-wing handles for leverage. The simplest lever corkscrew is the "waiter's friend"—so-called because it's the favorite among restaurant servers. It's got either a dual or single lever. Then there's the popular "rabbit" corkscrew with gripping handles on the sides and a top lever handle.

Before you can insert any corkscrew into the cork, you have to remove the capsule that surrounds the cork end of the bottle. In days gone by the capsules were made of lead, but producers today use foil or plastic. Cut them off with a small knife or the foil cutter that comes with many corkscrews. To avoid wine dripping over the edge of the foil, be sure to cut it low enough on the neck of the bottle—under the second lip of the bottle.

Through the Grapevine

unleashing the worm

The worm is not something you find at the bottom of a wine bottle as you do with certain tequilas. It's the curly metal prong found on most corkscrews that bores into the cork for removal. To avoid getting cork pieces into your wine while you're extricating the cork, be sure the worm doesn't go completely through the cork.

SERVING TIPS

Wine seems so temperamental. Coffee you serve hot, lemonade you serve cold. Easy. No fuss. With wine, different styles require different temperature. Personal preference is a factor. Should a wine breathe or be poured the moment it's opened? What's an attentive host to do?

Serving Temperature

Serving wine too cold masks its aroma and flavor. Unless it's a wine you want to disguise, you don't want to over-chill it. The cold also brings out any bitterness in the wine. On the other hand, serving a wine too warm will make it seem flat and dull and overly alcoholic.

The familiar rule for reds is to serve them at room temperature. But you have to take that advice in context. The rule was conceived when the "room" was in some stone castle with no central heating. Room temperature really means wine cellar temperature—somewhere between 50 and 55°F. Whites are served colder. Now, don't make yourself crazy with exact temperatures, but the following will give you some guidelines:

- *Sparkling wines and young, sweet white wines:* 40 to 50°F
- *Most whites:* 43 to 53°F
- *Rich, full-bodied whites:* 50 to 55°F
- *Light reds:* 50 to 60°F
- *Medium-bodied reds:* 55 to 65°F
- *Bold reds:* 62 to 67°F

Chilling a wine from room temperature will take from one to two hours in the refrigerator, depending on the final temperature target. You can reduce the time to about twenty minutes by submerging the bottle in a container of half ice and half water.

twenty-minute rule
White wines stored in the refrigerator are often too cold to serve, and reds stored at room temperature are often on the warm side. To compensate, follow the Twenty-Minute Rule. Twenty minutes before you serve your wines, remove the white from the refrigerator to warm it up a bit, and replace it with the red to cool that one off.

Let It Breathe, Let It Breathe

Letting a wine breathe means exposing it to the air. The oxygen begins to age the wine. In young red wines with high tannins, the exposure "softens" the tannins much like a few years of aging will do. You'll notice that as you sip a wine from your glass over time, the taste will subtly change. Some say the wine "opens up." Not all wines benefit from breathing. Most whites and Rosés don't need to breathe. As a general rule of thumb . . . if a wine needs no further aging, it doesn't need to breathe.

Some people have interpreted "breathing" as simply uncorking the bottle in advance of pouring. The truth is wine can't breathe in the bottle. The neck is just too small to let enough air inside. Studies involving wine experts have demonstrated that no one can really tell the difference between a wine that's been breathing in the bottle for minutes versus one that's been breathing in the bottle for hours.

If you really want to aerate your wine, pour it into your glass, swirl it around, and let it sit for a while.

When to Decant

A wine can require decanting for two reasons: It needs aeration or it needs to be separated from sediment that has settled with aging. For breathing purposes, simply pour the bottle of wine into a decanter for serving. And if it *really* needs to breathe (like it's just too tannic to drink otherwise), pour it back and forth between two vessels a couple of times.

Decanting to remove sediment is a more delicate process. Stand the bottle upright. Let it stand that way as long as possible so the sediment falls to the bottom of the bottle. A couple of days would be ideal, but even thirty minutes is helpful. Remove the cork without disturbing the sediment.

With a candle or flashlight standing next to the decanter, slowly pour the wine in a steady stream into the decanter. The light should be focused below the neck of the bottle. That way you'll be able to see the sediment the exact moment it appears. And that's your signal to stop pouring.

HOW TO MAKE A BARGAIN WINE LOOK EXPENSIVE

So maybe the wine didn't cost a fortune. But a few simple tips will help your whole party atmosphere seem a little more upscale.

- Serve the wine in a crystal decanter and use your best wine glasses.
- Serve with expensive cheese or fancy hors d'oeuvres.
- Act *as if:* let it breathe, swirl it, savor it.
- Use the lingo.
- Graciously accept their compliments.
- If they insist on knowing the label, tell them you'll send them the name via e-mail.
- Never apologize!

WINE AND YOUR DINNER PARTY

A dinner party puts you in control of events—barring any bad behavior on the part of your guests, of course. You orchestrate the meal—the courses, the ingredients, the preparation methods, the timing, the presentation . . . and the wine. Everyone will be eating the same foods—so you don't have to worry about matching the wine to six or eight or ten different dishes.

When you plan your food-wine matches, you can start either with the food or with the wine. If you're a particularly good cook—or if you have a special recipe that you want to showcase—that's the time to choose the wine based on how it will complement the food. If the food is to be the star, you'll want a wine in the "best supporting" role. If you have some exceptional bottles of wine that you've acquired and want to serve to an appreciative audience, you'll choose foods with some subtlety.

Wine Progression

A dinner party is like a staging a play. There's a sequence of events and a defined beginning, middle, and end. When your guests arrive, you can't just usher them into the dining room and make them eat. There's pre-dinner chitchat that requires a light accompaniment. Why not start with sparkling wine with hot or cold hors d'oeuvres? An aperitif is meant to stimulate the appetite, and bubbly fills the bill.

Through the Grapevine

oops!

If you discover fragments of cork in the bottle of wine, or if you discover, just minutes before serving, that your wine has sediment, there's no time to let things settle. You can filter the wine into a decanter through clean fabric such as muslin or through a paper coffee filter with no adverse effects.

Now, it's time for dinner. If you're serving more than one kind of wine with the meal, there's a general progression that works best for enjoyment. Serve white wines before reds, light wines before heavy ones, and dry wines before sweet ones. Yes, there are always circumstances that defy the rules. Say you have a light-bodied red and a full-bodied white. Which rule do you break? It's your choice. Or maybe you don't like red wines at all. There's nothing wrong with serving all whites.

In some circles, there's another rule: Drink lesser wines before better ones. The reasoning is that (like the play analogy), there's a big payoff at the end. It makes sense—but only to a point. After, say, the third wine, your guests will drink anything.

Quantities

How many bottles of each should you buy for your dinner party? With so many variables—your friends' passion for wine, the number of courses you plan to serve, if you plan to have a different wine with each course, the pace of the evening—there's no definitive answer. But there are guidelines. For total wine purchases, you can generally plan on one bottle of wine per person. If you're serving multiple wines, the following table breaks it down according to the number of wines and the number of guests.

**Dinner Party Wine Purchase Plan
(number of bottles of each wine needed)**

Number of Wines	4 Guests	6 Guests	8 Guests	10 Guests	12 Guests
2	2 bottles	3 bottles	4 bottles	5 bottles	6 bottles
3	1 bottles	2 bottles	2 bottles	3 bottles	4 bottles
4	1 bottles	1 bottles	2 bottles	2 bottles	3 bottles
5	1 bottles	1 bottles	2 bottles	2 bottles	3 bottles

Dessert wines are a separate consideration altogether. You can serve them as an accompaniment to a dessert—or *as* dessert. The serving size is much smaller, and the bottle size is half that of a table wine.

Wine Gifting

At some point, the tables will be turned, and you will be the one taking a bottle of wine to a dinner party.

The important thing to remember is to let your host know that it is a gift and not necessarily meant to be served that evening. To get him off the hook, say something like, "This is for you to enjoy later."

Through the Grapevine

it's all up to you

You've carefully selected your wines. You have a plan for which wine to serve with what food. As you greet your guests at the door, each one hands you a thoughtful gift of wine. What do you do? You say a gracious "thank you." You're not obligated to serve them— unless, of course, you want to.

If you would like to take a wine to be served at dinner, call the host ahead of time to let him know. That way you can take a wine appropriate for the food. And if you want your bottle oohed and aahed over, make sure the dinner will be a small gathering that will be properly appreciative.

WINE AND YOUR COCKTAIL PARTY

A cocktail party is any festive social event where people mingle and meet—whether it's a reception, an open house, or a mixer. "Cocktail" party implies that you'll be having . . . yes, cocktails with spirits and mixers and ice. In recent years, people have been drinking wine in place of cocktails—so it deserves a place at any cocktail party. The real question is whether you're going to offer a full range of drinks or whether you plan to limit the offerings to wine, beer, and nonalcoholic drinks.

The advantage to the latter is you don't have to worry about who's going to do all the mixing of drinks.

But it's your choice. Now you have to determine what wines to buy and how much.

Choosing the Wines

Here you're walking a fine line between a good-quality wine that you'll be proud to serve and a budget that you've established for solid reasons. A discussion with your retailer can be of real help here.

Consider the wine drinking preferences of your friends. Are they mostly white wine drinkers? Or red drinkers? Or a mix? Or, do they predominantly fall into the blush wine category? Even when you know your friends' preferences well, there's no way to predict with any certainty what they'll actually drink. (The night of your party your best red-wine-drinking buddy has switched to white!) All you can do is take your best guess.

When you don't know your guests well enough to know their preferences, it's safe (and thoughtful on your part) to stock both a red and a white. Cocktail parties deserve wines that are easy-drinking and that will be acceptable partners to the foods you'll be serving. While wines can be made in wide ranges of styles, here are a few suggestions:

- Sauvignon Blanc or Pinot Gris for easy-drinking whites
- Riesling for food-friendly white
- Beaujolais for light, easy-drinking red
- Pinot Noir for food-friendly red
- Tempranillo or Côtes du Rhone for smooth, down-the-middle reds

Calculating Quantities

The amount of wine you buy will depend on how many wine drinkers you expect and the length of the party. For ease of calculating, say you expect twenty wine drinkers for a three-hour cocktail party. Based on each person drinking a five-ounce glass of wine each hour, the equation looks like this:

20 (wine drinkers) × 5 (oz.) × 3 (hours) = 300 (total ounces) ÷ 25.4 (ounces in a bottle) = 11.8 (total bottles)

(Twelve bottles is a case. You can get a case discount!) Is the equation absolute? Of course not! You may want to adjust the numbers if your guests are heavy drinkers—or light drinkers. If it's an open house, guests may not stay for the full three hours. Party planning is not an exact science. If you're going to err, err on the side of overstocking. If you've selected your wine wisely (meaning you like it), leftovers won't go to waste.

For large parties, consider buying wine in containers larger than the standard (750 ml) bottles.

Magnums, for example, can offer savings. And with better wines now available in boxes, they, too, are an option. Here's a chart to help you in your calculations for different size containers.

Contents of Typical Wine Bottles and Containers

Size	Ounces	5-oz. Servings	4-oz. Servings
187 ml	6.3	1	1
375 ml	12.7	2	3
750 ml	25.4	5	6
1 L	33.8	6	8
1.5 L	50.7	10	12
3 L	101.4	20	25
5 L	169.0	34	42

WINE TASTING PARTIES

Definition of wine tasting party: solemn gathering of pompous individuals swirling, spitting, and uttering terms like "carbonic maceration" in reverential tones. Not! A wine tasting party can be anything you want it to be. Start with your intention. Do you want your event to be educational in nature so that your guests come away having learned something new about wine? Would you rather assemble a bunch of different wines and let your guests learn something by guzzling the wines on their own? There's room for both of these approaches—and everything in between.

"Traditional" Wine Tastings

Traditional wine tastings have a structure of sorts. And they need a leader—someone knowledgeable about the wines being served who can facilitate discussion and answer questions. If you're not comfortable in that role, it's not too difficult to locate someone who is. A phone call to a wine store or your favorite restaurant is usually all you have to do. (Make sure the person in the lead role has a sense of humor and is willing to go with the flow of your party.)

When you're planning your wine purchases, remember that a "tasting" serving is much smaller than the typical four- or five-ounce glass of wine. About two ounces is the norm. You can get twelve servings from a standard bottle. Buy a little extra just in case one of your guests wants to come back for another taste.

Food has a place at a wine tasting. It can be as simple as some unsalted crackers for guests to cleanse their palates between wines. At a structured tasting, you don't want the food to interfere. But an alternative "theme" would be a food and wine tasting to see how certain flavors—salty, fatty, or acidic—affect the taste of the wines.

Seat guests at a table with empty wineglasses in front of them—one for each wine if possible. Not everyone has that much stemware, but you can rent glasses if you want to go that route. Or you can limit the glasses to one or two per person. If you'll be tasting both reds and whites, splurge and go for two per person. In any case, have a pitcher on the table to rinse the glasses between wines. And, of course, a dump bucket for the water (or, heaven forbid, a wine).

Through the Grapevine

the invite list

Who do you invite? Invite anyone and everyone— regardless of their wine sophistication—who has an interest in sampling and learning about wine. How many wines do you serve? As many as you want—but five or six wines work well.

As with the sequence of wines for a dinner party, the general guidelines are white before red, light before heavy, and dry before sweet. In selecting the wines, you might want to consider a theme. Consider these traditional options:

- **Vertical tasting**—You serve several bottles of the same wine from the same producer, only from different vintages. For example, you could serve a Silver Oak Cabernet Sauvignon from Napa Valley from 1997, 1998, 1999, 2000, and 2001. The objective is to identify the wine's traits that appear from year to year—or the differences from one year to the next.

- **Horizontal tasting**—No, not a tasting while everyone is reclining. You serve the same kind of wine from the same year from the same general area but from different producers—say Pinot Noirs from Oregon's Willamette Valley from the 2003 vintage from different wineries.

- **Blind tasting**—You keep the identity of the wines secret while they're being tasted. That way no one is influenced by the reputation of a particular winery or region or vintage. Go ahead, include a jug wine in the tasting and see how it compares in the judging.

Through the Grapevine

sensual appeal

While educating your palate and narrowing your choices, here's some ways you can savor the sensuality of wine and extend your pleasure:

- Admire its color.
- Inhale its nose (smell).
- Savor its taste.
- Feel its texture.

Informal Tasting Parties

Informality suits some hosts (and guests) better than structure. But having a more casual wine tasting party doesn't mean that everyone can't learn—or sample—something new. A straightforward (and economic) strategy is to invite your guests to bring a bottle of wine and be prepared to tell the group a little something about it. Depending on your guests, the background information might turn out to be serious wine geek stuff or less-serious information.

Allot one wineglass per person and place water pitchers and dump buckets around the party rooms. As different wines are being poured, call on the guest who brought it to describe the wine and explain why she chose it.

Themes create a fun atmosphere for these less formal tastings, where your guests bring a wine related to the theme. Consider these, for example:

- **Kentucky Derby:** Leaping Horse Merlot, Equus Run Vineyard Chardonnay, Two Paddocks Pinot Noir
- **Academy Awards:** Marilyn Merlot, Francis Coppola Diamond Series Syrah
- **Anniversary:** Iron Horse Wedding, Cupid Chardonnay

A Wine Tasting Thesaurus

Remember: It's not about being clever, right, or wrong, but about expanding your palate, as well as finding ways to describe and remember your favorites. Encourage your guests to be eloquent about what they're tasting. Here are a few categories and adjectives to get you started:

- Aromas: Honeysuckle, clove, tobacco, cedar, grapefruit, black olive
- Flavors: apple, walnut, blackberry, oaky, peppery, citrus, chocolate
- Sweetness: From a tongue curling extra-dry to as rich as dessert
- Acidity: Mouth-pinching tart to as placid as water
- Tannin: As strong as coffee or as light as green tea
- Body: As rich as an expensive chocolate truffle or as light as a vanilla cupcake
- Texture: As creamy as butter, as thin as a wafer, or as hot as a pepper

- Balance: A symphony of flavors or a train wreck

HOLIDAY WINES

Holidays present their share of challenges—completely separate from the challenges of family dynamics. Certain foods are traditional. They're not always the foods you think about pairing with wines. Fried chicken on the Fourth of July. Tacos al carbon on Cinco de Mayo. Black-eyed peas on New Year's Day.

Picnic Wines

Ever notice how many holidays involve eating outdoors? A serious Cabernet just doesn't taste right when you're out in the sun frolicking around a pool or running to catch an overthrown softball. No, it's time to drink something that can take a good chill. Here are a few ideas:

- *Think white*: particularly a fruity white
- *Think pink*: a chilled, dry Rosé is made for picnics
- *Think light*: not all reds are big and bold (sure, chill the reds too)

Thanksgiving Wines

The problem with picking out a wine for Thanksgiving dinner isn't matching it to the turkey. It's all the other stuff. Every household has a well-established menu—with many of the recipes having been passed down for generations. You're not about to give up these foods anytime soon—cranberry-walnut mold, sausage-apple stuffing, orange-praline sweet potatoes, pumpkin cheesecake. With all the competing flavors, it's hard to know what to match.

Sometimes it's best to not worry at all. Pick out a wine that you know you like. It may not go with everything on the table—but what would? If it turns out to be a horrendous match, eat first and drink the wine later. There's always a solution. If you're looking for more concrete wine recommendations, some popular Thanksgiving wines include:

- Champagne
- Rosé
- Chenin Blanc
- Beaujolais
- Riesling
- Pinot Noir
- Gewürztraminer

THE PARTY'S OVER, NOW WHAT?

The party's over, and your sink is full of dirty dishes and dirty glasses line every tabletop and counter. There are wine stains on the tablecloth, a stash of garbage to be taken out, and at least five open bottles of leftover wine. What? Leftover wine? The best remedy for leftover wine is to drink it. But sometimes that's not the wisest move.

The wine has already started its inevitable decline. Its youth and vigor diminish with each passing minute. Oxygen and heat are the robbers. But even though you can't completely stop the premature aging, you can slow it down some. Recork the bottle and put it in the refrigerator. The cold will slow the chemical reaction that spoils wine. The advice goes for both white and red wines.

Wine bottles that are half full of wine are also half full of air. Removing the air is your goal, which you can accomplish with a set of marbles. Add them to the opened bottle until the level of the wine reaches the top. Recork and refrigerate.

But even with the best systems, you can't keep the wine forever. Usually, within days the wine becomes dull and flat. Wines have different abilities to withstand the ravages of oxygen and time. For a wine to stay in relatively good condition once it's been exposed to the air, it needs to be capable of aging in the first place. High-tannin reds are the most durable because they were meant to age. Whites won't last as long.

The Big Cleanup

The morning after a party in the light of day you discover . . . red wine stains! If you're like most hosts, you'll probably find wine stains on the tablecloth, the carpet, and your shirt. You'll find advice all over the Internet about ways to eliminate the stains, but your options for an effective resolution come down to two.

1. **Wine-Away:** It's a fruit-based formula in a spray bottle that you can use on carpet stains and as a presoak for laundry.

2. **A laundry presoak recipe from the UC Davis Department of Viticulture and Enology:** Mix equal parts 3 percent hydrogen peroxide and Dawn liquid dishwashing soap. Pour it on the stained fabric and launder as usual.

Now, you need to know a few basic tenets about cleaning your glassware. If you're washing the glasses by hand, use as little detergent as possible, the hottest water you can stand, and rinse, rinse, rinse. Sponges specifically designed for cleaning wineglasses are available to make the job easier. If you use a dishwasher, wash glasses only (not dishes or pots and pans), and don't use any detergent. In addition to leaving an odor, detergent can etch the surface of your crystal. Crystal is more porous than glass and easily absorbs tastes and odors.

chapter 11

WINE AND FOOD: WHAT GOES WITH WHAT

. . . .

A century ago, life seemed simpler. Everyone just drank their local wine and didn't fret about the "perfect match" for a meal. Then wine snobs came up with rules. First, the rules were as simple as red wine with meat and white wine with fish. But food got more complex and so did the rules. The truth is food and wine pairing is highly subjective and inexact. There are certain principles that can guide you. In the end, though, it's your choice. So relax and enjoy the experimentation!

. . . .

MR. CHEAP

ACQUIRING FINESSE

Food and wine are like a couple of ballroom dancers. Each one affects the performance of the partner. Sometimes they're slightly out of step. Sometimes their footwork meshes seamlessly. On occasion, they move as one and transform a simple dance into a moment of magic. And even when both partners have two left feet, it's still a fun exercise.

Food and wine, whatever their individual personalities, influence the way the other one tastes. A particular food can exaggerate or diminish the flavor of a wine. A certain wine can overwhelm a food.

Through the Grapevine

seeking synergy

When a food and wine combination has real synergy, the effect can be a third flavor experience that's greater than the two consumed separately. Admittedly, perfect unions are rare. And when they do happen, it's usually fate. So merely seeking two partners that are compatible is a reasonable strategy.

Wine as a Condiment

When wine geeks plan a meal, they choose the wine first and match the food to go with it. Most people start with the food and move on to the wine selection. Picking a wine is akin to adding a condiment. You'd hardly ask for a jar of mustard so you can slather some on your cheesecake. Matching wine and food is all about finding their common flavors and textures. You don't acquire that ability by memorizing a set of rules. You learn it through experimentation. Even though there are some matching principles that are good guides,

MR. CHEAP'S GUIDE TO WINE

everyone brings her own palate and taste preferences to the table.

If wine were a one-size-fits-all product, you could just pick food from column A of a chart and wine from column B. At fine-dining restaurants where wines are suggested for each menu item, the recommendations aren't just picked out of thin air. Before anything gets into print, the chef, the wine staff, and the wait staff all taste-test various wines with each course. They compare and discuss—and you can bet they don't all agree. No one will know how the decisions are finalized. But the process exemplifies the fact that even professionals have different viewpoints.

Too Many Variables

It used to be you could order a steak and French fries and a glass of Cabernet. Now there's fusion food with sixty-three ingredients in one preparation. Which ingredient do you match the wine with?

Not only ingredients affect the way foods taste; cooking processes do as well. You can have your food baked, boiled, broiled, grilled, poached, sautéed, fried, marinated, pasteurized, tenderized, and liquefied. Whew!

Now consider the wine: thousands of grapes, endless blending combinations, a dry-to-sweet continuum, oak or no oak, high alcohol/low alcohol, aged or not aged. It's enough to make you want to throw your hands up in defeat and just order a cup of coffee.

Think back to the days before you drank wine. Did you ever sweat it when a restaurant only had Pepsi . . . no Coke? Did you worry that a 7-Up might be a better match for your grilled cheese? Almost any choice you make is okay. It's not likely to ruin your meal. You can drink more or less any wine with more or less any food—and enjoy the experience.

red vs. white

Acidity is much more important in the taste and structure of white wines than red wines. In red wines, the taste balance depends on three components: alcohol, acids, and tannins—with tannins providing most of the structure. White wines have minimal tannins. So, there are only two components to consider: alcohol and acids—with acids providing the structure.

Matching Likes to Likes

There are some guiding principles that will point you in the right direction. The principles won't tell you *exactly* what to order, but they'll help you understand why some foods and some wines make compatible partners. The principles are based on the four tastes that the tongue can discern. And the idea is to match similar tastes in both the food and the wine.

Pucker Up

Foods that have a sour component are good matches for wines that are high in acid. A salad with a vinaigrette dressing and a fish fillet squirted with lemon both cry out for a high-acid wine. You're matching acid with acid. (Notice here that you're not matching the wine to the fish fillet itself or to the lettuce in the salad. You're taking into consideration the preparation.) Tomatoes, onions, green peppers, and green apples are examples of other high-acid foods. So, what wines are some potential high-acid food partners? Sauvignon Blanc, to start. Also the northern French whites of Sancerre, Pouilly-Fumé, Vouvray, and Chablis. The wines of Alsace and Germany generally have high acidity. The tannins often mask the acids in reds, but safe bets are Italian reds. (Why do you think Italian wines go so perfectly with tomato-based pasta sauces?) The following whites are listed from low acid levels to high acid levels:

Gewürztraminer (low)

Pinot Gris/Pinot Grigio (low)

Chardonnay (medium to high)

Champagne (medium to high)

Chablis (medium to high)

Chenin Blanc (high)

Riesling (high)

Sauvignon Blanc (high)

Sweet Things

The sweeter the food, the less sweet a wine will taste. Say you're eating a slice of roast pork with a glass of off-dry Chenin Blanc. The sweetness of the wine will be obvious. Top your pork with a pineapple glaze and your glass of wine will taste positively dry.

When you get to dessert, the rule-of-thumb is to drink a wine that's sweeter than your food. Even a moderately sweet wine can taste thin, unpleasantly dry, and even bitter when you pair it with a sugar blockbuster. Some suggested pairings include:

- Pear tart and Sauternes
- New York cheesecake and Muscat
- Bread pudding and late harvest Riesling
- Tiramisu and Port
- Dark chocolate mousse and Banyuls

spot a sweet wine before you buy it
Check the percentage of alcohol listed on the label—
generally, the higher the alcohol level, the drier the
wine, and the lower the level, the sweeter the wine.
That's because less sugar has been converted to alcohol during fermentation. Note: This rule doesn't apply to
fortified wines.

Bitter Buddies

When you eat food with a hint of bitterness and drink a wine with some bitterness (from the tannins that have not yet mellowed), they cancel out each other's bitterness. It's like they knock each other out in the first round of a head-to-head fight—and you're the winner. The following red wines are listed from low to high tannin levels:

Beaujolais (low)

Tempranillo (low)

Pinot Noir (low)

Merlot (low)

Sangiovese (medium)

Zinfandel (medium to high)

Syrah/Shiraz (high)

Cabernet Sauvignon (high)

Super Salt Me

Of course, you know there are no salty wines. But there are plenty of salty foods: ham, smoked salmon, oysters, teriyaki beef. To counteract a super salty meal, the best wine accompaniments are high-acid wines—especially sparkling wines. Acid cuts the saltiness—just like a squeeze of lemon does.

BEYOND TASTE

There's more to wine (and matching wine to food) than the four perceived tastes. Wine has power—to a greater or lesser degree. So do foods. One can easily overpower the other if the match-up isn't comparable. Both food and wine have texture and flavor intensity that is also part of the pairing equation. A big, brawny Amarone would overwhelm a dainty little broiled flounder at first sip. Conversely, a delicate Pinot Grigio wouldn't stand a chance of making an impression next to a fiery French pepper steak.

Alcohol is one of the contributors to a wine's sense of body and weight—the more alcohol, the more full-bodied the wine. So, even before tasting the wine, you can gauge its body by its alcohol content. A fuller-bodied wine will have more than 12 percent alcohol. Lighter-bodied wines will have less than 12 percent.

Cut the Fat!

Maybe you've heard that tannic wines will "cut the fat." It's true—but it's not what you think, hope, or pray for. Most unfortunately, tannic wines don't reduce the calories in that big, juicy steak you're coveting. (Curses, foiled again!)

Wine tannins are, however, attracted to fatty proteins. As you chew your steak, a coating of fatty proteins sticks to the walls of your mouth. When you sip a high-tannic wine, the tannin molecules attach themselves to the protein molecules—taking them along for the ride when you swallow. The best they do for you is to refresh your mouth and ready it for the next forkful of meat. Sorry, but you'll still need to pare down those portions to lose weight.

Spice It Up!

When you walk on the wild side with fiery dishes from Thailand or Mexico or India, choosing a wine can be tough. Your usual dry favorites somehow make the exciting heat of the food downright painful. Blame it on the alcohol. From a pain standpoint, you might be better off with a glass of milk—but, no, that's not an option. Wine it is.

A sweeter, lower-alcohol wine is a much more soothing match for spicy foods. Try a Riesling or Gewürztraminer or—gasp!—a White Zinfandel. With the heat turned down a notch, reds come into play. Pinot Noir and Beaujolais are definite candidates.

It's not foolproof, but one way to estimate a wine's tannin level is by its color. The lighter it is, the less tannin the wine is likely to have. It stands to reason: The longer the skins stay in contact with the clear grape juice during fermentation, the more color and tannins they impart.

WINE & CHEESE: THE MARRIAGE

Black and white. Horse and carriage. Gin and tonic. Laurel and Hardy. Wine and cheese. Classic matches, all. Wine and cheese both date back to ancient times—although cheese is the newer kid on the block at about 4,000 years. Wine and cheese both reflect their terroir and continue to mature as they age. With so much in common, their match-up is a natural.

An old wine merchant's saying goes, "Buy on an apple and sell on cheese." It means that wine sipped with a sweet, acidic fruit will taste thin and metallic. The same wine drunk with cheese will seem fuller and softer. But that doesn't mean that all wines pair well with all cheeses. Certain wine and cheese pairings have become traditional, pleasing most of the people most of the time—but, hey, they're pretty sensational so give the following classic pairings of wine and cheese a try:

- Goat cheese and Sancerre
- Brie and unoaked Chardonnay or Pinot Noir
- Mozzarella and Chianti
- Parmigiano-Reggiano and Barolor
- Gouda and Riesling
- Chèvre and Gewürztraminer
- Sharp Cheddar and Cabernet Sauvignon
- Stilton and Port
- Roquefort and Sauternes

Wine & Cheese: Pairing Basics

With the almost infinite number of wines and cheeses available, why stick to tradition? Experimentation is much more fun. The following guidelines may help in narrowing your purchasing options:

- The softer the cheese, the more it coats your mouth—requiring higher acidity in the wine.
- The sweeter the cheese, the sweeter the wine should be. Some mild cheeses, especially, have a sweetness that requires an off-dry wine. Dry wines may be perceived as acidic.
- Strong, pungent cheeses need strong wines. Extreme flavors in cheese work best with full-bodied red wines, sweet wines, and fortified wines.
- The harder the cheese, the higher level of tannins a wine can have.

CLASHES

A few baseball parks around the country have upgraded and expanded their concessions to include wine. Imagine having a hot dog with chopped onions, mustard, and sauerkraut and . . . oh forget it, just order a beer. Some foods are difficult to match with wine—not impossible, but problematic. It's pretty much accepted that certain foods are less than ideal candidates for wine partnerships, such as:

- Artichokes
- Olives
- Asparagus
- Spinach
- Chocolate
- Yogurt

When "difficult" foods are part of the menu, there's a way to get around the food-wine clash (assuming the difficult one isn't the *only* food on the plate): take a bite of something neutral, like rice or bread, between bites and sips.

All by Itself

On occasion, the wine is the difficult partner. There are some elements in wine that, when they're in full force, just don't taste good with food. Alcohol is one of them. It's a defining part of wine, but you'll enjoy drinking highly alcoholic wines far more by themselves. More often than not, lower alcohol wines are more flexible with foods.

Oak can be another problem. The toasty or vanilla flavor is a pleasant taste and a popular style. But oak in abundance is no friend of food. There's nothing wrong with enjoying a wine for what it is—all by itself.

FAIL-SAFE MEASURES

Too much analysis can be exhausting! Sometimes you just want to kick back, not think too hard, and enjoy a meal with wine and friends. Yes, there are strategies for those occasions that require easy answers.

Back to Its Roots

You're eating ethnic—German, Italian, French, Spanish. The simple wine solution comes from the home country. Europeans never made a big deal about matching food and wine. They just cooked the way they wanted and made wines that went well with their foods. Globalization of wine notwithstanding, Europeans still produce wines that taste good with their traditional fare.

Through the Grapevine

wine to the rescue!

If the dish you're serving is overly salty and you can't repair the food somehow, the wine can come to the rescue. Serve a wine on the sweeter side—perhaps a Riesling or Muscat. It will make the food taste less salty.

You're having paella? Bets are that a Rioja will be the best choice. Match your schnitzel and spaetzle with a German Riesling . . . or your osso buco with a Barolo . . . or your pot-au-feu with a Côtes du Rhone.

Of course, the system breaks down when the ethnic region of choice has no long history of winemaking—like Chinese, Thai, Cuban, and Indian. So, on to the next backup strategy.

Keep It Simple

Some wines are just naturally friendly. They make ideal dining partners no matter what you eat. You can choose one of them in any situation with the confidence that it will make a good match. It's as simple as the following 1, 2, 3.

1. Champagne or sparkling wine
2. Riesling, if you're in the mood for white
3. Pinot Noir, if you feel like a red

Friendly Wines

Some people have distinct wine preferences. Sure, maybe you think they need to walk on the wild side and try something new for a change. But the wine selection strategy that will be popular every time is to match the wine to the people.

Rarely has a meal been ruined by the wrong wine. If your friends drink exclusively Cabernet, or Shiraz, or White Zinfandel, make them happy by ordering their favorite. All right . . . you can't handle the White Zinfandel with your prime rib. That situation calls for two bottles of favorites.

COOKING WITH WINE

"I cook with wine; sometimes I even add it to the food." It's a funny line from W. C. Fields, but the underlying idea illuminates one of the surest ways to successfully match wine with a meal: Cook with the same wine you serve. The corollary to that piece of advice is don't cook with a wine that you wouldn't want to serve.

Only the Best!

The best chefs and home cooks wouldn't be caught dead shaking powdered Parmesan from a can or making do with a mushy cucumber. No, they turn out magnificent meals because they use the finest and freshest natural ingredients. And they know not to skimp on the wine as an ingredient. They may not use a grand cru for their sauces, but the wines they add to a dish are flavorful and worthy of drinking.

You've undoubtedly run across bottles of "cooking wine" as you've cruised the supermarket aisles. You know . . . right above the vinegars. That should tell you something. Sure, they're tempting because they cost so much less than a real bottle of wine. But stay away!

For one thing, the wine they started out with wasn't so hot. On top of that, they contain salt as a preservative—which makes them undrinkable. If you can't sip as you cook, where's the fun? (Their *undrinkability* makes them exempt from alcoholic beverages taxes—another reason they're so cheap.)

Salt in wine is redundant for cooking. It's not that table wine has salt, but wine heightens the natural flavor of foods—making the addition of salt unnecessary. In fact, be judicious with the saltshaker when you're also adding wine to a dish because the wine intensifies salty flavors.

Cooking Basics

Because wine has alcohol and acids and flavors all its own, it has certain cooking properties that you should be aware of.

- When using wine in dishes with milk, cream, eggs, or butter, add the wine first to prevent curdling.
- Add table wines at the beginning of cooking to allow the alcohol to evaporate and produce a subtle taste.
- Add fortified wines at the end of cooking to retain their full-bodied taste.
- To intensify a wine's flavor, reduce it. One cup of wine will reduce to ¼ cup when you cook it uncovered for about ten minutes.
- Using wine in a marinade will tenderize in addition to adding flavor.
- If you use wine in a recipe that doesn't call for wine, use it as part of the recipe's total liquid—not in addition.
- Unless the recipe specifies otherwise, use medium-dry to dry wines.
- Use white wine for light-colored and mildly flavored dishes and reds for darker-colored and more highly flavored dishes.

A dash of wine can really perk up a familiar dish. Try a splash of dry Sherry in a cream soup . . . or a bit of leftover Sauvignon Blanc in the pan when you've finished sautéing chicken . . . or a cupful of Chianti to add a robust flavor to Italian tomato sauce.

The most important rule of all: Don't add too much. Save some for sipping!

chapter 12

CHAMPAGNE & $PARKLING WINES

. . . .

What's the big deal? Who cares whether you call it Champagne or sparkling wine? The French do! They've protected the name Champagne by international treaty—which means, technically, only sparkling wines produced in the Champagne region of France can bear the name on the label (and you must capitalize it when you write about it). The treaty, by the way, doesn't apply in the United States.

. . . .

ALL ABOUT CHAMPAGNE

The term "champagne" has become generic in the United States to mean all bubblies. A hundred years ago Korbel used "champagne" on its labels. And so have others. It's been only in the last few decades that France has actively sought to protect the name. So, American marketers, with a century of tradition behind them, continue to call their product champagne. And most people—wine geeks included—do the same.

Through the Grapevine

bottle mania: deciphering *this* vs. *the*
Another sparkling process, the transfer method, is similar to *méthode champenoise* except that, instead of riddling and disgorgement, the wine is transferred after the second fermentation to pressurized tanks and filtered.
You have to read the fine print on the label to know.
"Fermented in *this* bottle" means traditional method.
"Fermented in *the* bottle" means transfer method.

The Bubble Machine

Champagne is more than a name. It's a universally adored beverage whose bubbles are created in a time-consuming and labor-intensive process. The technique, *méthode champenoise*, has six basic steps, as follows:

1. Grapes are fermented for about three weeks to produce still wines.

2. The producer blends his still wines according to what style he wants to achieve. This base wine is called the *cuvée*.

3. The wine is bottled and laid down. During the next nine weeks or so, a second fermentation takes place inside the bottle—producing carbon dioxide in the form of bubbles.

4. The wine is aged—anywhere from nine months to several years—according to the producer's specifications.

5. The bottles are rotated from a horizontal position to a vertical, upside-down position. This allows sediment to collect in the neck of the bottle close to the cork so that it can be removed easily and quickly. Rotating the bottles is called *riddling*.

6. The neck of the bottle is frozen and the sediment (in the form of a frozen plug) is removed—called *disgorging*. At this point, sugar is added (a process known as *dosage*)—the amount dependent on how sweet the producer wants the final product. And the bottles are recorked.

Spotting Cheap Bubbles

The traditional method of producing bubbles is expensive. The price you pay is a reflection of that. You can bet that when you buy a $5 bottle of sparkling wine, it was produced another—cheaper—way. The Charmat method (also known as bulk method, tank method, and cuve close) was likely used. It involves conducting the second fermentation in large, closed, pressurized tanks. With this process, you can produce a lot of wine in a short period of time—so the sparkling wine is ready to drink not long after harvest. Maybe only a few weeks.

Here's what happens:

1. Still wine is put into closed, pressurized tanks, and sugar and yeast are added.
2. Fermentation takes place, and carbon dioxide forms in the wine—producing a sparkling wine with an alcohol content higher than the base wine.
3. The wine is filtered under pressure to remove any solids.
4. Sugar is added to adjust the sweetness level desired, and the wine is bottled.

An even less expensive technique is sometimes used that simply injects carbon dioxide into the wine—like a carbonated soft drink. If that's the case, the label on the bottle will say "carbonated."

Through the Grapevine

tiny bubbles swim upstream

The bubbles will tell you something about what method was used. *Méthode champenoise* produces tiny bubbles that float upward in a continuous stream. Cheaper bubbles are large and random and don't last as long. Bubbles from carbonation aren't integrated into the wines like in Champagne—so they'll quickly disappear, much like the bubbles in your can of Coke.

Grapes Matter

To be "real" Champagne, only three grape varieties are allowed: Pinot Meunier, Pinot Noir, and Chardonnay. Pinot Meunier contributes a youthful fruitiness. Pinot Noir gives Champagne its weight and richness and is responsible for its longevity. Chardonnay adds lightness.

One of the most important decisions a Champagne-maker has to make is how to blend these grapes to make the base wine. Wines from the different varieties and vineyards are kept separate. The producer then blends the wines (including wines from past years) in varying proportions to create its distinct cuvée. This is what distinguishes the ultimate taste of one producer's Champagne compared to others.

Through the Grapevine

know your bubbly

You never know when you'll be on *Jeopardy!* and be required to answer a Champagne question, so here's some entertaining, and perhaps useful, trivia:

- A bottle of sparkling wine has about 49 million bubbles. The average diameter of a bubble is 0.5 mm.
- Way back when, the foil wrapped around the outside of the cage was lined with lead to prevent mice from eating the cork.
- The indentation at the bottom of a Champagne bottle is called a *punt.*

For sparkling wines produced by other methods, there are no such strict rules regarding grape variety. Generally speaking, tank-fermented bubblies tend to be fruitier than their Champagne counterparts.

LE HISTOIRE DE CHAMPAGNE

Until the mid-1600s, Champagne as we know it didn't exist. The region produced still wines, which were very popular with European nobility. But Champagne had yet to be "discovered." The Champagne region in northern France has a cold climate, posing problems for growing grapes and winemaking. Cold winters and short growing seasons mean that grapes had to be harvested as late as possible to get them as ripe as possible. That meant just a short time for fermentation because the cold temperatures of winter would put an end to the process. So the wines were bottled before all the sugar had been converted to alcohol.

Then spring would arrive, and fermentation would begin again—this time in the bottle. When the bottles didn't explode from all the pressure that had built up from the carbon dioxide inside, the wines had bubbles. To the winemakers of the time, bubbles signaled poor winemaking.

Through the Grapevine

finding the right angle

Madame Clicquot, a young widow who ran her husband's Champagne house after his death in 1805, was the first to solve the sediment removal problem. She cut a series of holes in her dining-room table so that the bottles could be positioned upside down at 45-degree angles. After several weeks of turning and re-angling the bottles, all the sediment collected in the neck.

Dom Pérignon, the Benedictine monk who's often called the inventor of Champagne, was one of those winemakers. He spent a good deal of time trying to prevent the bubbles. He wasn't successful, but he did develop the basic principles used in Champagne making that continue to this day. For example:

- He advanced the art of blending to include different grapes and different vineyards of the same grape.
- He invented a method to produce white juice from black grapes.
- He improved clarification techniques.
- He used stronger bottles to prevent exploding.

When Dom Pérignon died in 1715, Champagne accounted for only about 10 percent of the region's wine. But it was fast becoming the preferred drink of English and French royalty. A royal ordinance in 1735 dictated the size, weight, and shape of Champagne bottles as well as the size of the cork. Two historic Champagne houses came into existence: Ruinart in 1729 and Moët in 1743. By the 1800s, the Champagne industry was in full swing.

CHAMPAGNE HOUSES

Unlike other French wines that are named after growing regions, Champagnes are named for the houses that produce them. The houses, in turn, produce various brands of Champagne—called marques. The largest and most famous of the houses are known as Grandes Marques. You guessed it: big brands! Twenty-four of them belong to an organization that requires they meet certain minimum standards. Some of the more recognizable members include:

- Bollinger
- Pol Roger
- Charles Heidsieck
- Pommery & Greno
- Krug
- Louis Roederer

- Laurent-Perrier
- Ruinart
- Moët et Chandon
- Taittinger
- G. H. Mumm
- Veuve Clicquot-Ponsardin
- Perrier-Jouët

Beginning with Moët et Chandon in 1974, a number of French Champagne houses opened up shop in California. They produce sparkling wines the traditional way using the same grape varieties as in France: Pinot Noir, Chardonnay, and Pinot Meunier. The French-American productions include Domaine Carneros (owned by Taittinger), Domaine Chandon (owned by Moët et Chandon), Mumm Cuvée Napa (owned by G. H. Mumm), Piper Sonoma (owned by Piper-Heidsieck), and Roederer Estate (owned by Louis Roederer).

"Grower" Champagne

While some of the major Champagne houses have sizeable vineyard holdings, they still buy most of their grapes from the 20,000 or so small growers in the Champagne district. The small growers, who collectively own about 90 percent of the vineyards, are increasingly making their own Champagnes. About 130 of these grower Champagnes are available in the U.S. market (out of the 3,747 sold in France). You've probably never heard their names (they can't afford to pay for promotion and advertising like the big guys), but they offer high quality and bargain prices.

How do you recognize a grower Champagne? It's on the label. In the lower right-hand corner of the front label are two letters followed by some numbers. The letters that will tell you it's a grower Champagne are either

"RM" or "SR." Here are all the possible letters and what they mean:

- *NM (Négociant-Manipulant)*—The term means merchant-distributor. These are the big houses. They buy grapes in volume from independent growers.
- *RM (Récoltant-Manipulant)*—The term means grower-distributor. This is a grower that makes and markets its own Champagne.
- *SR (Societe de Récoltants)*—This is basically the same as grower Champagne. Two or more growers share a winemaking facility and market their own brands.
- *CM (Cooperative-Manipulant)*—This is a cooperative of growers who bottle their product together—although these wines can include purchased grapes.
- *RC (Recoltant-Cooperative)*—This means a grower sends its grapes to a cooperative to be made into wine. The grapes can be blended with other wines in the cooperative.

CHOOSING A CHAMPAGNE

A Champagne house establishes its reputation based on a particular style. Many factors influence the style—grape varieties, vineyards, blending choices, tradition. The objective of each house is to provide consistency from one year to the next. When you find a Champagne that you like, you can be sure it will have the same characteristics year after year.

Vintage Years

Champagne is produced every year. But "vintage" Champagne is only produced in the best years. Like in all other regions, some grape harvests in Champagne are better than others. In exceptional years, a house will decide to make its bubbly using only the grapes from that harvest—and will date the bottle with that year. In the years in between, the house blends wines from multiple years. It's termed *nonvintage* (NV). Blending across years is one reason you can expect uniform quality.

For a Champagne to qualify for a vintage date, at least 80 percent of the grapes used in producing it have to have been harvested that year. The other 20 percent can come from reserve wines from other years. A vintage Champagne has to age for three years before its release, but can be, and often is, aged longer.

Nonvintage Champagne represents most of a house's production—80 percent or more. They're usually lighter, fresher, and less complex than their vintage counterparts.

From Dry to Sweet

If Champagne were like most other wines, the grapes would be picked when they're perfectly ripe. They'd have plenty of natural sugar to be converted to alcohol. But, alas, that's not the case. The grapes are less than ripe. So the winemaker has to add enough sugar so the yeast will have adequate fuel to convert into alcohol. How much sugar is added is left up to the winemaker. And, needless to say, adding more sugar will make the Champagne taste sweeter. Then, there's another addition of sweetness at the end of the process right before bottling. Sweetness levels of Champagne are important parts of their styles. Progressing from dry to sweet, these are the levels:

- Extra Brut (also called Brut Sauvage, Ultra Brut, Brut Integral, Brut Zero)—driest of all but not a common style
- Brut—the most popular style and considered to be a good balance of sweetness to dryness
- Extra Dry (or Extra Sec)—dry to medium-dry
- Sec—medium-dry to medium-sweet
- Demi-Sec—sweet
- Doux—*very* sweet

Variations on a Theme

Pink Champagne! The accompaniment to romance! Rosé Champagne gets its pink color in one of two ways. The winemaker can leave the skins of the grapes in brief contact with the grape juice during the first fermentation . . . or add a little Pinot Noir wine to base the wine blend. People sometimes think of Rosé Champagne as sweet (maybe because they associate it with sweet blush wines), but it's definitely dry. It's available both as a vintage wine and as nonvintage.

Blanc de noir has a hint of pink, too. In wine terms, *blanc de noir* means "white wine from black grapes." This Champagne is made from just one of the permitted grapes: Pinot Noir or, less often, Pinot Meunier. It's fuller than Champagnes with Chardonnay in the blend. *Blanc de blanc* is another one-grape bubbly. It's Chardonnay all the way. It's lighter and more delicate than Champagnes that also include Pinot Noir.

Name Your Size

Have you ever noticed those super large Champagne bottles on display at wine stores and restaurants? Well, they're not just a marketing tool. They're real. Champagne is bottled in ten different sizes, shown below.

Champagne Bottle Sizes and Names

Measure	Size Equivalent	Servings	Popular Name
187 ml	quarter bottle	1	split
375 ml	half bottle	2	half
750 ml	standard	4	fifth
1.5 L	2 bottles	8	magnum
3 L	4 bottles	17	jeroboam
4.5 L	6 bottles	24	rehoboam
6 L	8 bottles	34	methuselah
9 L	12 bottles (1 case)	50	salmanazar
12 L	16 bottles	68	balthazar
15 L	20 bottles	112	nebuchad-nezzar

Only the half bottle, standard bottle, and magnum contain Champagne that's undergone the second fermentation in the bottle. And the three largest sizes are rarely made anymore. How many people must it take to pour from them?

Biblical Inspiration

Where do those bottle names come from, you ask? Sometime in the mid- to late 1800s, Champagne producers drew names from the Bible to distinguish their supersized, hand-blown bottles from the smaller 750 ml bottle.

- **Jeroboam** was named for one of the kings of Israel.
- **Methuselah** was named for the famous 969-year-old fellow.
- **Salmanazar** recognized the Assyrian king who ruled over Jerusalem.
- **Balthazar** commemorated one of the three wise men.
- **Nebuchadnezzar** was named for Balthazar's grandfather, the king of Babylon.

Champagne "splits" are handy because of their size—about a serving and a half. But, even though they are corked just like their bigger brothers, they don't keep as well. So drink them up right away before they lose their freshness.

CHAMPAGNE BY ANY OTHER NAME

The fact that a sparkling wine is produced outside of the Champagne region of France doesn't mean that it's inferior. It's just a little different. Some sparklers are made with the exact same grapes employing the same traditional method. They'll be different because of the terroir—the taste the earth has given to the grapes—and the blending choices of the winemaker. But even some experts have failed to recognize the difference between well-made bubblies from inside and outside the Champagne region.

French but Not Champagne

Even in the Loire Valley (so close to Champagne) they can't use the Champagne name on the labels of their sparkling wines. The region known, in part, for its use of Chenin Blanc grapes in Vouvray uses the same grapes for its bubblies. The effect is refreshing and creamy.

The eastern regions of France, including Alsace, are known for blending Pinot Noir, Pinot Blanc, and Pinot Gris for their sparkling wines. The bubblies turn out crisp. French sparkling wines produced outside of Champagne are labeled "Vins Mousseux."

Spanish Bubbly

It used to be called "Spanish Champagne." Then in 1970, the European Union banned the use of the term outside of Champagne. From then on Spanish sparkling wines have been known as *Cava*. The word is Catalan for "cellar," referring to the underground cellars where the wines are aged.

Through the Grapevine

metal detectives

Using atomic spectrometry to measure metal concentrations in the wines, researchers at the University of Seville in Spain correctly identified bottles of Champagne versus bottles of Cava 100 percent of the time. The measurements reflected the trace metal content in the soils where the grapes were grown. This technique could be used in the future to detect wine fraud.

To qualify as a Cava, the sparkling wine has to be produced in the traditional method using specified grape varieties. The list includes Chardonnay and Pinot Noir, which are used in the best wines, but producers still use the "big three" indigenous grapes: Macabeo, Xarel-Lo, and Parellada.

Cavas are usually light and crisp and inexpensive. For a taste treat, look for some of the following:

- Freixenet Cordon Negro Brut: $10
- Segura Viudas Aria Brut: $12
- Mont-Marcal Brut: $12
- Codorniu Brut: $12
- Paul Cheneau: $10
- Fleur de Nuit: $7

Italy Sparkles

Oh, so many bubblies to choose from in Italy . . . starting with Prosecco. It's made from the grape of the same name in the Veneto region of northeastern Italy. Prosecco comes both fully sparkling *(spumante)* and lightly sparkling *(frizzante)*. They're crisp and dry and inexpensive. They've become very popular, and you see more and more of them on restaurant wine lists.

Then there's the more familiar Asti (in the past known as Asti Spumante) made from the Muscat grape. Its second fermentation takes place in pressurized tanks in a modified version of the charmat method, and its taste is semisweet to sweet. Asti's cousin is Moscato d'Asti. It differs from Asti in that it's *frizzante* instead of fully sparkling, sweeter, lower in alcohol, and is corked like a still wine. Both should be drunk young and fresh.

Lambrusco is another Italian option. Most Americans know it as pink, semisweet, and *frizzante*. But it's also made white and dry.

german bubbly

Germany may not be known for sparkling wines, but it produces a whole lot of it. Most of it is consumed within its own borders. It's called *Sekt*, and it's made using the charmat method. Riesling is used for the better wines. If the bubbly has been made using just one variety, the grape name will be on the label.

Domestic Sparkling Wine

Sparkling wine is made almost everywhere still wine is made—the two largest producing states being California and New York. In California, particularly in the cooler climates of Sonoma and Mendocino counties, many wineries produce excellent bubblies. And not just the ones with ties to France. Names to look for: Gloria Ferrer, S. Anderson, Iron Horse, Schramsberg, to name just a few. While California gets most of the attention, sparkling wine has been a mainstay of New York winemaking since before the Civil War when French Champagne-makers were recruited there by local wineries.

Some sparkling wine recommendations from around the United States:

- Château Frank Brut (New York): $28
- Argyle Brut (Oregon): : $40
- Gruet Brut (New Mexico): $14

STORING AND SERVING BUBBLY

You never know when you'll need a bottle of Champagne. A friend drops in to say she's gotten (pick one): engaged, divorced, promoted, a raise, a diploma, a puppy. You need an appropriate way to celebrate: Champagne. You need an effective mood enhancer: Champagne. It's the universal beverage. Keeping a supply just makes good sense.

How to Keep It When You're Not Drinking It

Champagne is sensitive to temperature and light. Like other wines, it does best stored in a cool, dark place without big temperature fluctuations. You don't need an expensive cooling unit—a 50°F basement usually works fine. Champagne is ready for immediate consumption as soon as it leaves the Champagne house, but if you provide the right conditions for your bubbly, it'll last for three to four years—if you haven't drunk it by then.

And don't be afraid to keep it in the refrigerator. A couple weeks in the cold isn't going to hurt it.

"Popping" the Cork

First word of advice: Popping the cork wastes bubbles. The cork should be removed so the sound you hear is a soft "sigh." Removing the cork in this slow manner also reduces the risks of killing someone in the room. (After all, there are 70 pounds-per-square-inch of pressure in that bottle!) Here's a checklist for how to safely open your bottle of Champagne:

1. Remove the foil covering.

2. Stand the bottle on a counter for support. (It's safer than holding the bottle in your arms and possibly pointing it at someone.)

3. Get a towel. Keep one hand over the top of the cork with the towel between your hand and the cork. Untwist the wire cage. Remove the wire.

4. Keep the towel on top of the cork with one hand and put your other hand on the bottle at a point where you have a good grasp.

5. Turn the bottle—not the cork. You'll feel the cork loosen a bit. Keep a downward pressure on the cork as it completely loosens and finally releases.

6. Hold the cork over the opened bottle for a few seconds to ensure the Champagne doesn't escape.

7. Pour!

Pour slowly. Because of the bubbles, the liquid rises quickly . . . and you can end up with overflow (and wasted Champagne!) before you know it.

Through the Grapevine

chilling shortcut

Bubbly is best served around 45°F. It will take three to four hours in the refrigerator to cool a bottle. But you can quick-chill your Champagne in about twenty minutes by immersing the bottle in ice water. It's faster than ice alone. Half ice and half water in an ice bucket is the way to go.

Drinking Vessels

You've undoubtedly seen the sherbet-style glasses that were popular in the 1950s. Now that "retro" is so chic, the glasses are everywhere. Buy them if you want . . . but don't use them for Champagne. Long-stemmed flutes are the glassware of choice for sparkling wines. The elongated shape and slight narrowing at the rim enhance the flow of bubbles and keep them from escaping. There's no need to chill the glasses. If you do, they'll just fog up and cloud your view of the bubbles.

A couple more "words to the wise" about glasses. If there's soap residue on the glasses, you may experience lots of foam that doesn't subside—caused when the carbon dioxide meets the detergent. To prevent this, always rinse the glasses thoroughly when they're washed. And keep in mind that dusty glasses will destroy the bubbles.

CHAMPAGNE LEFTOVERS

On the rare occasions that the bottle of Champagne hasn't been emptied, your main objective is to save the bubbles for another day. Your best bet to preserve the effervescence is a Champagne bottle stopper. It's made of metal with a spring and special lip to grab the rim of the bottle. They're available in most kitchen stores and in wine stores in states that allow them to sell wine accessories. A good backup procedure is to wrap the bottle opening with two layers of plastic wrap and secure it with a rubber band.

For quality Champagnes, you can usually stick the uncorked bottle back in the refrigerator overnight and still have bubbles in the morning. What happens is that inert and heavy carbon dioxide gas from the bubbles forms a protective layer on top of the wine, preventing oxidation and containing the bubbles below. But a day—maybe two—is about as long as the protection will last.

Alas! You open the refrigerator door, and all the bubbles have disappeared. There are still last-ditch efforts you can make to try to revive the patient. One is to put a raisin in the bottle. Another is to put a paper clip into the bottom of each glass before you pour the Champagne into them. It's always worth a try. Remember, even without bubbles, Champagne makes an excellent cooking wine!

chapter 13

DESSERT & $PECIALTY WINES

. . . .

Now that we've covered traditional wines and Champagne—and all the other sparklers—Let's talk about dessert and specialty wines. The popularity of sweet wines has gone through cycles. One day they're on top of the heap, next day they're out of favor. Regardless, they've had a resurgence in popularity of late.

. . . .

MR. CHEAP

A SWEET HISTORY

Sweet wines go back to ancient times. The most acclaimed wines in Rome were sweet and white. The ancient wine-makers let the grapes raisin on the vine or they dried them on straw mats to concentrate their flavors. The resulting wines were sweeter and stronger—and more durable to withstand transportation to outlying areas.

Through the Grapevine

bittersweet?

Not all wines that start out with the grapes being dried on mats are sweet. Far from it! Recioto della Valpolicella Amarone—better known as just "Amarone"—is made in the same way except that it's fully fermented to produce a completely dry wine. The name *Amarone* translates to "strongly bitter."

In the Middle Ages, Venice and Genoa made sweet dried-grape wines that they exported to northern Europe. Sweet wines appeared in other parts of the world too. Tokaji from Hungary and Constantia from South Africa were highly prized sweet wines that were on every royal table in Europe.

LATE HARVEST AND NOBLE ROT

Legends, by definition, aren't totally reliable. But here's one version of the creation of late harvest sweet wines: In 1775, a messenger was sent to Schloss Johannisberg in Germany's Rheingau region to give the official order to start harvesting the grapes. He was robbed on the way and delayed. By the time he got to the wine estate, the grapes had begun to raisin on the vine. They were picked anyway and produced astonishingly delicious sweet wine. There's evidence that sweet late harvest wines had already been produced throughout Europe in the previous century. But it makes a colorful story.

Late Harvest Wines

The term *late harvest* means that the grapes were picked late into the harvest season when they were ripened past the sugar levels required for ordinary table wine. The extra ripening time—which can be weeks—adds sugar but also adds significant risk from rain, rot, and birds. The high sugar content of the grapes can translate into a wine that's sweet or a wine high in alcohol—or both.

Through the Grapevine

finicky fungus

Botrytis is a finicky fungus. Under the wrong conditions, "gray rot" forms instead and spoils the grapes. If the weather is unremittingly hot and dry, the fungus won't develop at all. The result is a sweet but much less complex wine.

Late harvest wines are known for their rich, honeyed flavors. Riesling grapes (the variety of most late harvest wines) have the ability to develop high sugar levels and, at the same time, maintain their acidity. That's why they can be unbelievably sweet without being cloying. The acidity also helps these white wines to age as well as they do. Late harvest wines aren't limited to Riesling. They're also made from Sauvignon Blanc, Gewürztraminer, Sémillon, and even Zinfandel.

Noble Rot

While the Germans have their legend for "inventing" late harvest wines, the French have their own legend for the famous Sauternes wines. It seems a château owner told his workers not to pick his grapes until he got back from a trip. By the time he returned, the grapes were infected with a fungus that shriveled them. Despite their disgusting appearance, the grapes were picked and turned into wine. The taste was so exquisite that the owner declared his grapes would thereafter always be picked after the fungus had arrived.

The friendly fungus of the legend is *Botrytis cinerea,* known affectionately as noble rot. It helps the water in the grape evaporate and causes the grape to shrivel, leaving a more concentrated sweet juice.

Good Noble Rot?

A wide range of grapes can benefit from the positive effects of noble rot—Riesling, Chenin Blanc, Gewürztraminer, Sauvignon Blanc, Sémillon, and Furmint among them. Three areas in particular are historically famous for their botrytized wines.

- **Sauternes**—The wine by the same name is made mostly from Sémillon but usually includes some Sauvignon Blanc and sometimes Muscadelle. The sweet Sauternes aren't necessarily made every year. If the grapes don't ripen properly and if *Botrytis* infection doesn't set in, the winemakers may decide to produce dry wines instead and label them as Bordeaux.
- **Germany**—German winemakers use Riesling to produce their Beerenauslese and Trockenbeerenauslese wines.
- **Hungary**—Tokaji (also referred to as Tokay) comes from an area around the town of Tokaj. They're made primarily from Furmint grapes.

ICE WINES

Who ever would have thought up the idea of making wine from frozen grapes? It was one of those divine accidents. The "discovery" of ice wine dates back to the winter of 1794 when producers in Franconia, Germany, had frozen grapes on their hands and decided to go forward with the pressing. When they finished, they were startled by the high sugar concentration of the juice.

When grapes freeze, the first solid to form is ice. As the grapes are crushed, the ice is left behind with the other solids—the skins and seeds. To give you an idea of how concentrated the juice is: If the sugar content of the juice was 22 percent when pressed normally, it would be 50 percent or more after freezing and pressing.

In order for the grapes to freeze, they have to be left on the vine well into the winter months. Waiting for them to freeze can be risky business. If the weather doesn't cooperate and the grapes don't freeze, a grower can lose his entire crop. Harvesting takes place by hand in the early (and necessarily cold) morning hours when acidity levels are at their highest. Pressing produces only tiny amounts of juice—one reason for the extremely high prices of ice wines.

Who Makes Ice Wine

Germany and Austria were the traditional producers of ice wine (*Eiswein* in German), but in the last ten years Canada has taken over as the largest producer. Canadian winters are much more predictable. The Canadian versions use a variety of grapes besides Riesling, including some lesser-known varieties like Vidal Blanc and Vignoles.

In Canada—as in Germany and Austria—the making of ice wines is strictly regulated. There are standards for sugar levels, temperature at harvest, and for processing. Ice wines are produced in the United States—particularly in Washington State, New York's Finger Lakes region, and states around the Great Lakes like Michigan and Ohio. No such strict standards exist for domestic ice wines.

Some producers use an alternate method for making ice wine: They stick the grapes in the freezer before pressing them. The lower prices for these ice wines reflect the easier production.

PORT

The origins of Port—the great fortified red wine—goes back to the seventeenth century trade wars between England and France. The British had developed a real affection for the wines of Bordeaux, but import bans and high taxes forced the English merchants to look elsewhere for their red wines. The "elsewhere" was Portugal. They found wines to their liking inland along the Douro River. To make sure that the wines arrived back in England in good condition, the merchants added Brandy to stabilize them before shipping them.

Then in 1678, a Liverpool wine merchant sent his sons to Portugal to search out some wines. They ended up at a monastery in the mountains above the Douro where the abbot was adding Brandy *during* fermentation—not after. The alcohol stopped the fermentation process, leaving a sweet, high-alcohol wine. The wine became known as Porto—and, to this day, that designation on the label means that the contents are authentic Port. And that, as legend has it, was the beginning of Port as the world has come to know it.

What's in a Name?

Kind of like the rules about the name *Champagne,* to be called *Port* the wine has to come from a specific place—the Douro region of Portugal. Port-style wines are made all over the world, but they're not true Port.

Through the Grapevine

all roads lead to portugal

Port-style wines are made in areas such as California, Washington State, Canada, Australia, and South Africa. If they're labeled as Port, they also have to include the area of production. Producers tend to use grapes from their own areas in the blends—not necessarily the traditional grapes of Portugal.

English merchants set up trading companies in the city of Oporto to ship the wines to England. That's one reason so many of the Port producers have English names.

Top Port Producers

The quality Port producers that are of British descent are Cockburn, Sandeman, Croft, Taylor, Syington, Dow, Graham, and Warre. The "Grand Dame" of Port is Ferreira. Equally good Port houses are Fonseca and Quinta do Noval.

The regulations governing Port's production allow eighty different grape varieties to be used. In practice, though, it really comes down to a handful. The most important ones are:

- Tinta Roriz (the same as Spain's Tempranillo)
- Touriga Nacional
- Tinta Barroca
- Tinto Cão
- Touriga Francesca
- Bastardo
- Mourisco

The Nature of Ports

Ports come in a head-spinning number of styles. Most of them are red and sweet. But not all. The style varies according to the quality of the base wine, how long the wine ages in wood before it's bottled, and whether the wine is from a single year or blended with wines from other years.

Port is aged in large wooden casks over a number of years. It reacts with oxygen through the surface area and through the wooden stoves. The aging process in bottles is much slower because there's almost no oxygen. Ports are either wood Ports or bottle-aged Ports—except when they're a little bit of both. Is all this becoming perfectly clear?

Top of the Line: Vintage Port

A Vintage Port is aged in the bottle for most of its life. It spends only two years in cask. When it's bottled at the age of two, it hasn't had a chance to shed its harsh tannins. That's left to happen in the bottle, which—without oxygen—is going to take a *very* long time. It

requires at least twenty years of aging and can continue
to improve for decades after that.

$OMMELIER CENTS

it was a singularly good year

Single Quinta (meaning vineyard property) Vintage
Ports emerged in the 1980s and have become very
popular. They're made from grapes from single-vineyard sites, and they're usually produced in undeclared
years. The producer has deemed the quality of the wine
from that location to be exceptional. Expect a price tag
to match.

What really distinguishes a Vintage Port from all
the others is that the grapes come from the best vineyard
sites in a singularly outstanding year. And that doesn't
occur every year. On average, a Vintage Port will be
made three years out of ten. The wines that are produced
in the off years (the *undeclared*) years go into the other
types of Port.

Vintage Port is bottled unfiltered and unfined—so,
once opened, it requires decanting to remove the sediment that's accumulated. The wine should be consumed
in one sitting.

Late-Bottled Vintage Port (LBV)

LBVs are probably the next best thing to Vintage
Port. They're vintage dated and made from a producer's
best grapes, but they come from undeclared years. LBVs
spend from five to six years in cask to speed up the aging
process. They're ready to drink when they're released.

Tawny Port

Tawnies are aged in wood for years—as long as
forty—until they fade to a tawny color. They're a blend

of wines from several years and are ready to drink immediately. Once opened, they can retain their vitality for a few weeks.

A Tawny Port will often be categorized by age, which appears as "10 Year Old," "20 Year Old," "30 Year Old," and "40 Year Old" on the label. The number is really an average age because older, more complex wines are blended with younger, fruitier wines. Colheita Ports are Tawny Ports from a single year (*colheita* is Portuguese for "vintage").

Ruby Port

Ruby Port is one of the least expensive Ports. It's bottled while it's still young—with only two to three years in wood. It retains its dark ruby color and has a limited shelf life. "Reserve" or "Special Reserve" indicates it's been aged longer.

White Port

White Port is produced just like red Port except it's made from white grapes—principally Malvasia and Donzelinho. Producers sometimes make a drier style by lengthening the fermentation period. The drier whites are typically served as an apéritif.

SHERRY

Say "Sherry," and you immediately think of England. But Sherry—the underrated and misunderstood fortified wine—comes from Spain. It's produced in the Jerex region from three main grape varieties: Palomino for the dry Sherries and Pedro Jimenex and Moscatel for the sweet wines. Making Sherry involves a number of steps and many twists and turns.

Relying on a Finicky Yeast

Once the base wine is made and put into barrels, a yeast called flor forms on the top of the wine. Not all the wines in the barrels are susceptible to the yeast, and the yeast will only grow with proper temperature and humidity. The flor does a couple of things. If influences the flavor—adding a tangy character to the wine—and it creates a protective layer like a crust on top of the wine so no further oxidation can occur. How well the flor develops determines the style of the Sherry. When the flor fully forms, the wine will be dry and crisp. These will be fino Sherries.

Occasionally—and mysteriously—the flor will begin to form and then stop. This may happen in one out of every hundred barrels. The dry and complex Sherry that results is called Palo Cortado.

Wines that don't form the flor at all are the *olorosos*, which have a rich, raisin flavor. They develop with full exposure to the air.

Fortifying and Blending

The next step is to fortify the wines with a clear Brandy, which boosts their alcohol content—and then onto one of the most fascinating blending operations in all of winemaking, known as the *solera system*. Because most Sherries aren't vintage dated, there is the need to make the wines consistent from year to year. To achieve this, wines from many years—and sometimes wines from as far back as a hundred years—are blended together.

Through the Grapevine

let's go nutty

Manzanilla is an extra-dry fino Sherry. It's light and delicate with a slightly salty flavor derived, more than likely, from the seaside town where it's aged. Amontillado is an aged fino that's rich, almost amber in color with a nutty flavor.

Imagine rows and rows of casks all stacked on top of each other—up to fourteen tiers. The oldest wines are on the bottom and the youngest on top. Producers remove about a quarter to a third of the wine from the bottom barrels and bottle it. They replace what they just removed with a wine from the next oldest, one tier up. This cascading of Sherry from the younger to the older continues all the way to the top. By blending all these wines together, you get a product that's consistent and homogenous.

Sherry to the nth Power

Sherries start out as either a fino or an oloroso (with the very few exceptions of the Palo Cortado). Then it gets complicated. Sometimes aging will change the character of a Sherry so it no longer fits into its initial category. And sometimes the Sherries are sweetened, producing still different styles. Among the sweet Sherries are:

- Paul-Cream—a lightly sweetened fino
- Cream Sherry—a heavily sweetened oloroso
- Brown Sherry—an extremely sweet and dark oloroso

MADEIRA

Madeira is just about indestructible. While almost all other wines can't take heat and motion and won't last more than a couple of days once the bottles are opened, Madeira can survive all those things. In fact, Madeira thrives on heat. That's how it's made.

Madeira is a Portuguese island off the coast of North Africa. It was perfectly situated in the Atlantic to become a thriving port for ships traveling to South America and around Africa to Asia. Ships loaded wine onboard for the long journeys. The only problem was that the wines were undrinkable by the time the ships arrived at their destinations. So alcohol, distilled from cane sugar, was added to stabilize the wines.

After enough trips, it was discovered that the wines tasted better after the voyages than before. And, further, the Madeira that had made a roundtrip was better than Madeira that had traveled only one way.

Shippers began putting wine in the holds of ships for the sole purpose of developing their flavors. It eventually got too expensive—so winemakers had to come up with other ways to simulate the journeys. Subjecting the wine to heat did the trick.

Madeira usually starts out as a white wine. After fermentation it spends at least three months in heated tanks or rooms—or exposed to the sun. As the wine bakes, sugars become caramelized to an amber color, and the wine is oxidized. The term is *maderized*.

The different styles of Madeira are named after the grapes they're made from, as follows:

- Sercial—the driest style, tangy with high acidity
- Verdelho—medium-dry with nutty flavor
- Bual (or Boal)—rich, medium-sweet with raisin flavor
- Malvasia (or Malmsy)—sweet and concentrated

Sercial and Verdelho are appropriate as apéritifs. The sweeter two are dessert wines. When grape names don't appear on the label, the style will be indicated in a more straightforward fashion: dry, medium-dry, medium-sweet, and sweet.

chapter 14

WINE AND YOUR HEALTH . . . WHY WINE IS ALWAYS A BARGAIN!

. . . .

One Sunday evening in November 1991, 33.7 million Americans watched *60 Minutes* reporter Morley Safer reveal an odd phenomenon in France. The French people, he said, ate high-fat, cholesterol-laden foods—like cheese, butter, eggs, organ meats—yet they had a much lower rate of heart disease than supposedly healthier-eating Americans. He went on, "Obviously, they're doing something right—something Americans are not doing. Now it's all but confirmed: Alcohol—in particular red wine—reduces the risk of heart disease."

. . . .

THE FRENCH PARADOX

This phenomenon became known as the French Paradox and, within four weeks of the television show's broadcast, U.S. sales of red wine soared by 40 percent. The report prompted a change in thinking of wine as a toxin to wine as a potential healer. And it encouraged research projects to investigate how wine consumption affects our hearts, lungs, brains, bones—and our overall health.

Does the French Paradox still stand up? While the research is ongoing, studies conducted around the world seem to confirm that wine and other alcoholic beverages—consumed in moderation—reduce the risk of coronary heart disease by 20 to 40 percent.

WINE VS. BEER AND SPIRITS

With all the research analyzing the effects of wine, beer, and spirits on various parts of the body, the jury is still out on whether the health effects are due entirely to the components in wine or to alcohol in general. Some studies have shown wine to have influence independent of alcohol. Still other studies have produced the same results regardless of the source of alcohol.

The impacts on health resulting from wine and other alcoholic beverages may differ, researchers believe, because of the way they're consumed—not necessarily their inherent properties. Consider the following:

- Wine enthusiasts tend to drink wine with meals rather than on empty stomachs.
- Wine drinkers tend to sip more slowly.
- Wine drinkers tend to spread their drinking out over an entire week rather than binge on weekends.

The upshot is that, for wine drinkers, the alcohol may be absorbed more slowly and over a longer period of time. And the resulting health effects might be different.

WHAT THE STUDIES SAY

It's hard not to be confused by all the scientific studies that are released every day. The information is often complicated, incomplete, or even contradictory. What is universally accepted is that excessive consumption of alcohol creates serious health risks—liver damage and hypertension among them. At the same time, evidence is emerging that moderate wine consumption can be beneficial in a number of areas. Recent studies show that drinking one glass of red wine every day may help protect against certain cancers and heart disease, and may even have a positive effect on cholesterol levels and blood pressure.

While many scientists now agree that drinking one glass of red wine a day for women and up to two glasses of red wine a day for men may decrease the risk of heart disease, cancer and stroke, excessive or binge drinking,

WINE AND YOUR HEALTH . . . WHY WINE IS ALWAYS A BARGAIN!

definitely does not produce the same benefits. In other words, when it comes to red wine: more is not better.

exactly how much is "moderate" consumption?

Other countries define "moderate" consumption more liberally—in the United Kingdom and European Union, for example, "sensible limits" are two to three glasses of red wine per day for women and three to four glasses for men. The U.S. government, however, defines "moderate consumption" as no more than two drinks a day for men and one drink a day for women.

Heart Disease and Stroke

Individuals who drink alcoholic beverages in moderation have a lower risk of coronary heart disease than heavy drinkers or abstainers. It doesn't seem to matter whether the alcohol comes from an expensive Bordeaux, a Bud, or a dirty martini. The alcohol increases the level of "good" cholesterol (HDL) in the body. HDL acts like a detergent, removing excess fat in the blood and carrying it to the liver where it's metabolized.

Much the same holds true for preventing strokes. In addition to increasing the level of good cholesterol, the blood is prevented from clotting—which reduces the risk of ischemic strokes.

Diabetes

Observational studies indicate that diabetes occurs less often in moderate drinkers than in abstainers. The Harvard School of Public Health conducted a study of 100,000 women over fourteen years. The women were divided into three levels of alcohol consumption. After factoring for family history of diabetes and smoking, the results showed that the women who drank moderately and regularly had a 58 percent lower risk of developing diabetes than abstainers. Women who drank more or less still had a 20 percent lower risk than nondrinkers. Results applied to both wine and beer drinkers—but not spirits drinkers.

Alzheimer's Disease and Dementia

Studies from different areas around the world have shown that moderate drinkers are less likely to develop dementia. Research on elderly participants have documented that the moderate drinkers performed better on memory and cognitive tests than nondrinkers.

In a Danish study designed to screen for signs of mental decline, researchers found that participants who drank at least one glass of wine a week were much less likely than those who drank no wine to develop dementia. Beer and spirits failed to produce the same results.

Bone Mass

It was once accepted that alcohol lowers a woman's bone mass, leading to osteoporosis. However, a couple of recent studies have indicated otherwise. One study was conducted to determine the effect of alcohol consumption on the bones of elderly women and how that might differ from the use of estrogen-replacement therapy. Moderate drinkers, it showed, had the greatest bone mass followed by light drinkers and followed, finally, by nondrinkers.

In a study of twins in England, it was determined that moderate-drinking individuals had significantly greater bone mass than their infrequently drinking twins.

Longevity

The American Cancer Society conducted a survey of a half million people over nine years to examine "total mortality"; that is, the risk of dying of any cause. The risk was greatest among abstainers and people who drank six or more alcoholic beverages a day. Moderate drinkers (who had one-half to two drinks a day) had a 21 percent lower risk than nondrinkers.

THE RULES OF CONSUMPTION

Current thinking is that the health effects of alcohol consumption depend on both how much you drink and your drinking patterns. Because many of the biological effects of alcohol are short-lived (lasting only twenty-four hours), the best advice seems to be, if you're going to drink, do it moderately every day. Don't save it up for weekend partying.

Through the Grapevine

potent exceptions

Drinking alcoholic beverages is always *inappropriate* at certain times—like when you're going to be behind the wheel of a car. Or when you're pregnant. Heavy drinking—on a regular basis—causes fetal alcohol syndrome, so the conservative approach is to completely avoid drinking during pregnancy.

A recent University College London study of civil servants found frequent drinking was more beneficial for cognitive function than drinking only on special occasions. Research on hypertension at the Worcester Medical Center in Massachusetts determined that men who drank monthly had a 17 percent lower risk of cardiovascular disease than nondrinkers. Weekly drinkers had a 39 percent lower risk. And daily drinkers had a 44 percent lower risk.

Although the explanations have yet to be conclusively determined, consuming alcoholic beverages with food seems to be beneficial as well.

BEYOND ALCOHOL: OTHER HEALTH COMPONENTS IN WINE

Wine in some cases goes beyond just the alcohol in producing health benefits. Recent research focuses on identifying the specific components in wine that are responsible and explaining how they work. Much of the emphasis is on antioxidants. Oxidation of cholesterol in the blood has been linked to clogged arteries, blood-clot formation, and tumor growth. Antioxidants inhibit that oxidation.

Through the Grapevine

beyond grapes

The antioxidants found in wine come from the grapes. But the antioxidants aren't exclusive to grapes. The same ones are also found in allium vegetables—onions, leeks, garlic, shallots—and broccoli, spinach, blueberries, strawberries, tea . . . and chocolate!

Antioxidants in wine come in the form of phenolic compounds such as tannins and flavonoids. The flavonoids in red wine are especially powerful—more than twenty times more powerful than those in vegetables.

The antioxidant that's getting most of the attention these days is resveratrol. Resveratrol is produced in the skins of grapes in response to fungus attacks and stress. Because red wines are fermented in contact with the skins, they acquire more resveratrol than white wines and carry more potential benefits than either white wines or other alcoholic beverages.

247

Grapes from cold, damp climates that have to "fight" harder to survive produce more resveratrol than those in warm climates. And grapes that are more sensitive to growing conditions—like Pinot Noir—seem to have more resveratrol than their hardier counterparts—like Cabernets.

WINE AND WEIGHT LOSS

Confusion reigns when it comes to the effect of wine (and other alcoholic beverages) on weight loss. Wine has plenty of calories—about 100 calories a glass. So it would just seem logical that if you cut out wine, you'd lose weight. But there's no evidence that giving up wine on your diet will necessarily help you shed the pounds. In fact, a major U.S. study revealed that dieters who gave up their alcohol lost no more weight than those who kept drinking.

Wine's calories come primarily from the alcohol. Most of the sugar was converted to alcohol during fermentation. The exceptions are fortified dessert wines that have both high sugar *and* high alcohol content. You may notice, too, that even some slightly sweet wines—like White Zinfandel and Riesling—have more calories than fully dry table wines.

Through the Grapevine

add it up

Calories in wine are directly related to the alcohol content. To determine the number of calories in a glass of wine, multiply the percentage of alcohol (found on the label) by the number of ounces you pour into the glass, and multiply that by 1.6. Example: *13 (percent alcohol) × 5 (oz.) × 1.6 = 104 total calories*

There are numerous variables that affect how wine will fit into your weight-loss regimen, for instance, it may depend upon the following:

- Whether you use wine to replace food or drink it in addition to food.
- How much wine you consume.
- How your body is genetically predisposed to process alcohol.
- What foods you eat.
- How much exercise you get.

Wine and Carbohydrates

Wine labels are now allowed to include calorie and carbohydrate counts. Low-carb diets have been so popular that some wine companies were quick to jump on the bandwagon of "low-carb" wines. Wines, of course, are inherently low-carb. The residual sugar left over after fermentation determines the number of carbohydrates. Use the following chart to compare the amounts to other beverage choices.

Carbohydrate Counts in Selected Beverages

Beverage	Amount	Carb Grams
Red Wine	1 glass	0.4–2.3
White Wine	1 glass	0.8–1.0
Dessert Wine	2-oz. glass	7.0
Beer	1 bottle	9.0–12.0
Light Beer	1 bottle	3.0–8.0
Spirits	1.5-oz. shot	0–0.1
Coca Cola	1 can	40.0
Diet Coke	1 can	0.3

TOO MUCH OF A GOOD THING

So you've had one drink too many, and now you're plagued with a queasy stomach, shaking hands, and a pounding headache . . . the can't-keep-your-balance and I'm-gonna-be-sick kind of feeling. Without a doubt, you overdid a good thing.

Through the Grapevine

metabolize this!

The alcohol that has not been metabolized can be measured in breath and urine as "blood alcohol concentration" (BAC) or "blood alcohol level" (BAL). BAC peaks within thirty to forty-five minutes after consuming a drink. BAC is measured as a percentage. In most states, .08 percent is considered legally drunk.

When you wake up with a hangover, you always promise that you won't do that again, and yet the next time someone opens a bottle of great wine…you're off and running. For the sake of science, let's take a sobering look at how your body reacts to ingesting alcohol.

How Wine Moves Through the Body

Once you take a sip of that incredible Amarone, it goes into the stomach, where 20 percent of the alcohol is absorbed. The rest moves on to the small intestines, where most of the rest is absorbed. The alcohol is delivered to the liver, where enzymes break it down. Now, the liver can only process a limited amount of alcohol at a time—about one drink an hour. When you consume more, the alcohol is in a holding pattern—in your blood and body tissues—until the liver can metabolize some more.

you really are frying your brain!
Here's the really bad news: Heavy drinking causes
brain shrinkage! Overindulging has more lasting effects
than hangovers. The brain shrinks as a natural part of
aging, but excess alcohol speeds it up and causes damage to the brain's frontal lobe—the part that controls
cognitive functions.

Men and Women Process Alcohol Differently

Some physiological differences between men and
women are obvious. Others are less apparent. The ways
their bodies process alcohol are different—even when
they're the same size. Consider the following:

- **Women have less body water—52 percent
  compared to 61 percent for men.** The man's
  body will be able to dilute the alcohol more
  readily than a woman's body can.
- **Women have less of the liver enzyme (dehy-
  drogenase) that breaks down alcohol.** So a
  woman will metabolize alcohol more slowly.
- **Hormonal factors have an impact.** Premen-
  strual hormones cause a woman to get intoxi-
  cated more quickly. Also, birth control pills
  and estrogen medications will slow down the
  rate that alcohol is eliminated from the body.

THE HANGOVER

A hangover is the body's reaction to alcohol poisoning
and withdrawal. It starts from eight to twelve hours after

WINE AND YOUR HEALTH . . . WHY WINE IS ALWAYS A BARGAIN!

your last drink. The severity may vary from one person to the next—but, fundamentally, it's based on how much you consumed. The symptoms might be as mild as thirst and fatigue—or as acute as headache, depression, nausea, and vomiting.

There are few things you can do to cure a hangover. Time and water are your best friends at that stage. But there are some measures you can take to prevent a hangover. (Drinking less goes without saying!)

- Before you start drinking: Eat something high in fat. It will delay absorption of the alcohol.
- While you're drinking, drink a glass of water between each glass of wine. It will keep you hydrated and minimize intoxication.
- While you're drinking, snack, snack, snack.
- Before you go to bed, eat something salty to replenish what the alcohol has flushed out of your body. And then drink *more* water.

HEADACHES

Here it goes again. You're sipping a perfectly exquisite Cabernet, appreciating its maturity and its velvety texture and—WHAM! The throbbing starts and doesn't abate. Where did that headache come from?

You've heard all the rumors about sulfites. Surely, they're the culprits. They must be evil. After all, the label on the wine bottle has a bold, cautionary warning: "Contains sulfites"!

Relax . . . or relax as much as you can while you're experiencing excruciating pain. You're going to have to find another scapegoat. Chances are, your headache derives from something other than sulfites. Only

1 percent of the general population is actually allergic to sulfites—usually individuals with asthma or those on steroid medications. If that's you, you'll more than likely develop rashes, abdominal pain, or extreme breathing problems from the wine.

The Sulfite Story

In wine, as in other foods, some sulfites are naturally present. Sulfur is abundant in various forms in all living things. In winemaking, manufactured sulfites are added to wine to prevent bacterial growth and to protect against oxidation. The practice of using sulfites as a preservative isn't new—and it's done by winemakers worldwide. Only when their wines are sold in the United States do they have to be labeled with the sulfite warning. It's the same wine—different label.

The amounts of added sulfites are small—measured in parts per million (ppm). The legal limit for some foods goes as high as 6,000 ppm. For wine the maximum allowed is 350 ppm, but most wines contain much less—typically from 25 to 150 ppm. In general, the less expensive the wine, the more sulfites it will have. And whites will have more than reds.

The law says that if a wine contains 10 ppm or more total sulfites, the label must carry the sulfite warning. To be labeled a "no sulfite wine," it can contain no more than 1 ppm. Because those wines are very perishable, they should be drunk soon after release.

More sulfites are added to white wines than to reds. White wine grapes are fermented after their skins have been separated. Red wines are fermented in contact with their skins. In addition to imparting color, the skins pass on tannins during fermentation, which act as a natural preservative.

The Blame Game

Okay, don't blame it on the sulfites. But the headache isn't just your imagination. So what causes it? There are plenty of suspects, but it's not so easy to pick out the exact one. Some culprits include:

- **Histamines**—These are chemical substances found in aged and fermented foods like wine, cheese, and salami and found naturally in eggplant. Histamines can dilate the blood vessels in your brain. Red wines usually have a higher level of histamines.

- **Tyramines**—These are chemical substances found in cultured foods such as cheese and yogurt; fermented foods like wine, dark beer, and soy sauce; and chocolate, vanilla, nuts, and beans. Tyramines can constrict the blood vessels in the brain.

- **Congeners**—These organic compounds are the by-products of the fermentation process that gives wine its characteristic flavor. There are hundreds of them present in wines in varying amounts depending on the type of wine. When congeners enter the bloodstream, your immune system recognizes them as poisons and releases cytokines (the same molecules that fight off the flu) to eliminate them. Generally, darker beverages (red wine, bourbon) have more congeners than lighter ones (white wine, vodka).

- **Prostaglandins**—These are naturally occurring pain-producing substances in your body. Dilation of the arteries triggers their release. They're also thought to be responsible for migraine headaches.

- **Sensitivities to elements in wine production**—Some people are extremely sensitive to woods. The soil where the grapes are grown contains various types of chemicals and could be a factor. That's why you might be able to drink a Cab from Napa, for example, without any negative effect—yet get a headache from a Cab made in Australia.

WINE-HEALTH CHALLENGES

Real wine enthusiasts, rather than casual drinkers, look for ways to keep wine as part of their daily lives—in spite of occasional "challenges." Headaches are major challenges, but life presents others that are more easily managed.

Purple Teeth

You may not be a professional wine taster who samples a couple hundred wines in a day's time, but you're not totally immune to the discoloring effects of red wine. The stains usually aren't permanent and disappear when you brush your teeth. But if you're really into reds big time, you may notice that the purple color doesn't completely go away. A trip to the dentist for a professional whitening procedure is the best answer. However, there are some measures you can take to prevent and fix the situation, as follows:

- Wait an hour or so after drinking wine to brush. The high acidity in wine can leave your teeth sensitive to abrasion. Brushing prematurely could damage your tooth enamel.

- Drink water between sips of wine. It will help eliminate the acid.
- Before brushing, rinse with a little bicarbonate of soda.
- Use a fluoride rinse two to three hours before wine tasting.

No Alcohol, Please

When you *really* like wine but have to stay away from alcohol, what do you drink? Are alcohol-free wines a good alternative? When it comes to their taste, you're the only one who can decide. No wine drinker has ever been fooled into believing the alcohol-free version was the real thing. But producers have been coming closer to reproducing the tastes.

The wines are fermented normally. Then the winemaker removes the alcohol. The exact process of removing the alcohol varies from one producer to another. The wines are reconstituted with grape juice or water and bottled.

One thing you should know is that alcohol-free wines are not necessarily totally free of alcohol. Check the label. You'll usually find the level of alcohol at .5 percent.

Get the Lead Out

Lead crystal is beautiful. And wine looks particularly elegant in crystal glasses and decanters. But, over time, wine can absorb some of the lead. It's not going to be much of a problem drinking a Riesling out of your grandmother's goblets for an evening. But storing a Sherry in a decanter over several weeks is something to avoid. For new crystal, soak it in vinegar for twenty-four hours and then rinse. And stay away from harsh detergents, which can increase the release of lead.

A FEW SELECT
RESOURCE BOOKS

The Wine Report, Tom Stevenson, Penguin Group, London, 2005. *Gourmand Magazine* dubbed this annual report the "best wine book in the world in 2004 and 2005." It's chock full of information, updated annually. Blankets the world and holds a treasure trove of information. Generates from Europe so has Euro prices.

Oz Clarke's Pocket Wine Guide. Webster's International Publishers, London, 2005. Prominently recognized as one of the world's top enophiles (wine lovers), Oz Clarke publishes an annual guide to his 1,600 favorite wines for the year. Handy because it discusses current varietals and lists the wines alphabetically, but may appeal to the higher-end bargain-hunter who wants to sock in some savory finds.

Oz Clarke's Encyclopedia of Grapes, A Comprehensive Guide to Varieties and Flavors, Harcourt, Inc., London, 2001. Everything you wanted to know about grapes and more!

The Good Life Guide to Enjoying Wine, Ray Johnson, The Writer's Collective, Cranston, RI (USA), 2006. A compilation of answers to questions that will help budding wine enthusiasts to develop confidence in their own taste and discover places to develop their palate and nose for bargains.

Oldman's Guide to Outsmarting Wine, 108 Ingenious Shortcuts to Navigate the World of Wine with Confidence and

Style, Mark Oldman, Penguin Books, NYC, 2004. Easy to read and packed with useful information.

Jancis Robinson's Concise Wine Companion, Oxford University Press, Oxford, UK, 2001. A dictionary of wine terms that will cover everything you ever need to know.

PRONUNCIATION GUIDE

Albariño ....ahl-bah-REE-nyoh

Alsace.................................ahl-SASS

Beaujolais ....boh-zhuh-LAY

Blanc de noir ....blahngk duh NWAHR

Bordeaux ....bor-DOE

Bourgogne........................boor-GON-yuh

Brouilly..............................broo-YEE

Brut....................................BROOT

Cabernet Sauvignon..........ka-behr-NAY SAW-vee-nyohn

Campania ....kahm-PAH-nyah

Cava..................................KAH-vah

Chablis...............................shah-BLEE

Champagne ....sham-PAYN

Chardonnay ....shar-doh-NAY

Châteauneuf-du-Pape ....sha-toh-nuhf-doo-PAHP

Chianti ....kee-AHN-tee

Chinon ....shee-NOHN

Cinsault.............................SAN-soh

Cognac ....KOHN-yak

Côte de Nuit ....koht duh NWEE

Côte d'Or...........................koht DOR

Côtes du Rhone ....koht deu ROHN

Dolcetto.............................dohl-CHEHT-oh

Douro.................................DOO-roh

Doux ....DOO

Eiswein...............................ICE-vine

Fumé Blanc ....FOO-may BLAHNGK

Gamay ....ga-MAY

Gewürztraminer ....guh-VURTS-trah-mee-ner

Graves ....   GRAHV

Krug...................................KROOG

259

Lambrusco	lam-BROO-skoh
Loire	LWAHR
Madeira	muh-DEER-uh
Merlot	mehr-LOH
Muscadet	meuhs-kah-DAY
Muscat	MUHS-kat
Nebbiolo	neh-BYOH-loh
Nouveau	noo-VOH
Orvieto	ohr-VYAY-toh
Penedès	pay-NAY-dahs
Pinot Blanc	PEE-noh BLAHNGK
Pinot Grigio	PEE-noh GREE-zhoh
Pinot Gris	PEE-noh GREE
Pinot Noir	PEE-noh NWAHR
Pouilly-Fuissé	poo-yee fwee-SAY
Pouilly-Fumé	poo-yee few-MAY
Quinta	KEEN-tah
Riesling	REEZ-ling
Sancerre	sahn-SEHR
Sangiovese	san-joh-VAY-zeh
Sauternes	soh-TEHRN
Sauvignon Blanc	SAW-vee-nyohn BLAHNGK
Sec	SAHK
Sémillon	seh-mee-YAWN
Semillon	SEH-meh-lon
Shiraz	shee-RAHZ
Sommelier	saw-muhl-YAY
Spumante	spoo-MAHN-tay
Syrah	see-RAH
Tastevin	taht-VAHN
Valpolicella	vahl-paw-lee-CHEHL-lah
Vin de pays	van duh pay-YEE
Vouvray	voo-VRAY
Zinfandel	ZIHN-fuhn-dehl

appendix C

A GLOSSARY OF WINE TERMS

acidity: Naturally occurring acids in grapes that are vital components for the life, vitality, and balance of all wines.

aging: Maturing process of a wine to improve its taste.

alcohol: The major component in wine. Also known as ethyl alcohol.

appellation: The official geographical location where the grapes used in the wine are grown.

aroma: The smell of a wine.

astringent: The puckering sensation in the mouth attributable to the tannins and acids found in some wines.

austere: A tasting term that is used to describe young wines that have not yet developed a discernable aroma.

balance: A tasting term that describes how well a wine's components complement each other.

barrel: A container used to store or ferment wine.

big: The term used to describe wines that are full of flavor and with high levels of tannins, alcohol, and grape flavor extracts.

bite: A result of good levels of acidity (especially in young wines).

bitter: Unpleasant taste that registers at the back of the tongue.

blanc de blanc: A white wine—most often sparkling—made exclusively from white grapes.

blanc de noir: A white or slightly tinted wine—and usually sparkling—made exclusively from red grapes.

blend: The technique of mixing wines of different varieties, regions, and barrels from different years.

body: Perception of fullness or texture in the mouth due primarily to the wine's alcohol.

bottle aging: Allowing wine to acquire complexity, depth, and texture in the bottle.

bouquet: The combination of flowery and fruity aromas that come from the alcohols and acids in a wine.

breathe: Allowing air to mix with a wine to develop its flavor.

brut: Dry style of Champagne and sparkling wine.

capsule: The protective cover of tin, lead, aluminum, or plastic that is placed over the top of a bottle of wine to insulate the wine from outside influences.

Cava: The Spanish term for sparkling wines made using the traditional Champagne method.

character: A wine's features and style.

clarity: The appearance of wine that has no cloudiness.

clean: Wines that are straightforward and have no unpleasant odors or flavors.

cloudy: The opposite of clarity; wine that is visually not clear.

complex: Nuances of flavors of a wine often achieved with aging.

cork: The spongy material from the bark of the cork tree used to seal wine bottles.

corked: Wines that have the smell of wood "dry rot" resulting from a defective cork.

crisp: Wines with good acidity and taste without excessive sweetness.

cru: French term meaning "growth."

cuvée: Blend; in the production of Champagne, cuvée is the specific blend of still wines used as a base for Champagne.

decanting: Pouring wine from a bottle into a carafe or decanter.

depth: Wines with full-bodied, intense, and complex flavors.

disgorging: Removing sediment from a bottle of Champagne following secondary fermentation.

dry: Opposite of sweet. All the sugar from the grapes has been converted to alcohol during fermentation.

earthy: Flavors derived from the soil where the grapes have been grown.

enology: The study of wine and winemaking; also oenology.

extra dry: Champagne classification where there is a slight perception of sweetness.

fat: A big, soft, and silky wine that fills the mouth.

fermentation: The process that turns grape juice into wine. The enzymes in the yeast convert sugar into alcohol and carbon dioxide.

fining: Clarifying young wine before bottling to remove impurities.

finish: The aftertaste or impression a wine leaves after it's swallowed.

fortified wine: Wine whose alcohol content is increased by adding brandy or neutral spirits.

fruity: The flavor or aroma of fruits in wine.

hard: An abundance of tannin or acidity.

ice wine: Extremely sweet wines made from grapes that have been frozen on the vines prior to harvest; also called Eiswein.

late harvest wine: Wine made from ripe grapes left on the vine for periods in excess of their normal picking times, resulting in an extreme concentration of sugar.

lees: The sediment of yeasts and small grape particles that settle in the barrel as wine develops.

maceration: Technique of fermenting uncrushed grapes under pressure to produce fresh, fruity wine.

magnum: A bottle holding 1.5 liters or the equivalent of two standard bottles.

meritage: Term used for both red and white American wines that are produced by blending traditional Bordeaux grape varietals.

nutty: A fine, crisp flavor often found in sherries and fine white wines.

oak: The flavor imparted to wine by barrel aging. It can be best described as a toasty or woodlike flavor. Sometimes a vanilla flavor will be imparted by fine oak to the wine.

oxidation: Exposure of wine to air, which causes chemical changes and deterioration.

pigeage: A French term for the traditional stomping of grapes by foot.

press: The piece of equipment used to gently separate grape juice from grape skins.

punt: The indentation at the base of a wine or Champagne bottle, which reinforces the bottle's structure.

reserve: A term without a legal definition in the United States but often used to designate a special wine.

richness: Rich wines have well-balanced flavors and intrinsic power.

sec: A term, when applied to Champagne, that describes a relatively sweet wine. Used in the context of still wines, the term means dry—without any residual sugar.

secondary fermentation: The process of converting still wine into Champagne that takes place in the bottle. In the production of still wines, the term is sometimes used in place of malolactic fermentation.

sommelier: French term for "wine waiter."

spumante: The Italian term for fully sparkling wines as opposed to those that are slightly sparkling—frizzante.

tannin: Substance found naturally in wine from the skin, pulp, and stalks. Tannins are responsible for the astringent quality found in wine, especially red wines.

Tannins form the basis for the long life of wines and, while they can be overpowering in young wines, with bottle aging, they tend to become softer.

terroir: Literally the "soil." A French term referring to the particular character (aromas and flavors) of a given vineyard—or even a small part of that vineyard.

thin: Wines that lack fullness, depth, and complexity.

varietal: A wine named after the grape from which it is produced. In California, for instance, a wine labeled "Pinot Noir" must by law consist of at least 75 percent Pinot Noir grapes.

vineyard: The place where grapes are grown.

vinification: The process of making wine.

vintage: Harvest year of grapes and the resulting wines made from them. Ninety-five percent of the wine in a vintage-designated bottle must be from grapes harvested in that year.

viticulture: The practice (art, science, and philosophy) of growing grapevines.

woody: In most wines this is an undesirable condition indicating that there is a taint of some type from defective wood or an overuse of new oak.

yeast: Naturally occurring, single-celled organisms found on the skins of grapes that are the primary promoters of fermentation. In the fermentation process, yeast turns sugar into alcohol and carbon dioxide.